CW00968467

The Practical Horse Herbal

Natural Therapies for Your Horse

Victoria Ferguson

HORSES for COURSES

CARLTON
BOOKS

DISCLAIMER

The information in this book is not to be used in place of veterinary care and expertise.
No responsibility can be accepted by the writer or publisher for the application of any of the enclosed information in practice.

THIS IS A CARLTON BOOK

First published in Australia in 2000
by Victoria Ferguson

This edition first published by Carlton Books Ltd
An imprint of the Carlton Publishing Group
20 Mortimer Street
London
W1T 3JW

10 9 8 7 6 5 4 3 2 1

Copyright © 2002 by Victoria Ferguson
Colour illustrations of herbs by Beth Greedy
Pen and ink illustrations of horses and herbs by Pauline McCarthy
Pen and ink illustrations of herbs by Holley Ryan
Typesetting by Pauline McCarthy

A catalogue record for this book is available from the British Library.

ISBN 1-84222-565-0

Printed and bound in Dubai.

FOREWORD

Victoria's book comes at a critical time. Health care providers for both humans and animals are realising the public's desire to use less toxic treatments when challenges to health occur. The general mood is shifting. People are wanting to understand what other health options are available. They are looking for treatments that will nurture the body, unlike many of the medical procedures and drugs available currently.

But the public has a dilemma. Although there is a wealth of information available on dietary herbal remedies and other alternative health strategies, how should they source this information and how can they be confident and know that the information they find is appropriate?

This book provides reliable concise information on nutrition and basic herbal remedies for many of the routine problems that horse owners will encounter. It is information they can depend on to enable them to help care for their horses themselves in many instances. In the future, optimal health care for horses will routinely involve a group of health care professionals including the Herbalist, the Homeopath, the Chiropractor, the Acupuncturist and the Veterinarian. Congratulations to Victoria in facilitating one of the first steps toward more holistic health care for horses.

Dr Ian Bidstrup M V Sc : Cert Vet Acu : Cert Vet Chiro
Dr Joanne Watkins M V Sc : Affiliate Member of the
American Academy of Veterinary Homeopathy

ABOUT THE AUTHOR

Victoria Ferguson grew up on a sheep station in Central Queensland. She went mustering with her father and started riding in shows at the age of 5 years. She has been addicted to horses ever since. Well known in the equestrian industry, Victoria has competed successfully with hacks, showjumpers, eventers, campdrafters and dressage horses. With her Grand Prix dressage partner Gamekeeper, Victoria was selected on the long list for the Australian team to the 1990 World Championships. She is an Equestrian Federation of Australia Level 2 Dressage Instructor. Under her Horses for Courses banner, Victoria trained and sold many Olympic discipline horses all round Australia. She also worked in the beef cattle industry for many years as a publicist and journalist.

Victoria completed her herbal medicine training with the eminent Australian herbalist and author, Dorothy Hall. She combines this knowledge with a lifetime of hands on experience with horses to work as an equine herbalist. Victoria is a columnist in the equestrian press on herbs for horses. Performance and pleasure horses all over Australia and overseas benefit from her natural health programs.

DEDICATION

This book is dedicated to the memory of "Gamekeeper" (1977-1996) The following words were written by my friend and fellow competitor Debbie Stewart to commemorate his passing. "Gamekeeper, the Grand Prix partner of Victoria Ferguson, inspired a generation of dressage competitors with his international paces and superior ability. Everyone watched him. His 14 year career began as a showjumping reject due to his bucking and bad behaviour. Victoria recognised his brilliance and persisted throughout his career. International judges acclaimed his abilities and huge overseas offers often followed their visits. Gamekeeper's beautiful chestnut presence and fiery Thoroughbred temperament will be sadly missed, but his inspiration will live on."

ACKNOWLEDGEMENTS

To my father, a good horseman, who encouraged me to make horses and riding part of my life; and to my mother, who encouraged me to read widely and practise the skill of writing.

With special thanks to my friend and assistant, Elm, for her help in making this book happen; to the illustrators Pauline McCarthy, Beth Greedy and Holley Ryan and to Ian Bidstrup, Joanne Watkins, Andrew McLean and Sandy Parker for their expert and willing assistance.

CONTENTS

LIST OF COLOURED PLATES

    ALOE VERA ; CHAMOMILE ; COMFREY ; DANDELION
    ECHINACEA ; FENNEL ; GARLIC ; NETTLES ; RED CLOVER
    ROSEHIPS ; WORMWOOD ; YARROW

1 HORSES ... NATURAL HERBALISTS

Cast your mind back some 6,000 years... and imagine the time when the modern horse was saved from extinction through its domestication by Eurasian steppe dwellers.

An appreciation of the evolution of the modern horse and the circumstances of its domestication provides today's horse owners with answers to keeping their charges healthy in mind and body.

Firstly the horse is able to survive on a wide variety of readily available foods. Secondly horses are one of only ten species of mammals (out of 4,000) that have been successfully domesticated. It seems that they discovered how convenient it was to graze on the crops cultivated by man and at the same time gain some protection from predators close to human habitation. Thirdly their relatively non-territorial mating habits as well as their social structure of understanding signals of dominance and submission facilitated the final stage of domestication. This enabled horses to be bred in captivity and used as draught and riding animals as opposed to being slaughtered for meat.

Man together with the horse established not only agriculture but civilisation itself. With the advent of mechanisation the horse was once again saved from extinction through the remarkable expansion of equestrian sport.

Paradoxically, the current world population of 60 million horses is probably greater than at any other time in the co-evolutionary history of man and horse.

Today's domesticated horses still have those same instincts and genetic structure which dictates their dietary and social needs. Because of their domestication there has been no genetic pressure on them in the past few thousand years for those patterns to be altered.

Instead the pressure is coming from man.

In their relationship with man at the present time the

modern horse has lost many of the benefits of domestication. A large proportion of the horse population suffers from deprivation of their natural behaviour especially instinctive foraging, unmounted exercise and socialisation. It is these factors which are causing a great many of today's health problems. This includes selection for fads, fashions and dollars which results in negative genetics.

Horses, like other animals, now have diseases and ailments mostly unknown in the wild, caused by man's ignorance of the unchanging laws of nature and his over-commercialisation of the earth.

INSTINCTIVE FORAGING

As a grazing animal the horse proliferated throughout the great grasslands on a large variety of plants and grasses. They ranged through huge tracts of land searching for beneficial feeds. Instinct led them to eat plants that helped them survive. Many medicinal plants grew on these steppes, savannahs and prairies.

At that time man lived close to nature and their survival depended upon learning the different properties of plants. "Early herbal medicine developed by the trial and error method. Medicine men and women tested plants on themselves and their animals. Some took herbs and became stronger and were revered as shamans for their magical healing abilities. Others died in the testing of new plants, but the information was passed on to other family members.

The secrets of the healing qualities of plants were kept within the families." (1)

The domestication of the horse gave humans the responsibilities of feeding, caring for and healing these animals, using the very same plant medicines they used on themselves.

After less than 100 years of pharmaceutical medicine,

the new millennium is seeing a widely popular revival of herbal medicine - for all species - not the least being the horse.

Happily today the "secrets" of healing plants are universally available, through published works dating back to the time of the Pharaohs and from increasing numbers of practitioners trained in the use of herbal medicine.

THE HEALTHY HORSE

Whilst it is obvious that domestication has afforded many horses an apparently comfortable lifestyle without too much effort - imagine working on average one hour a day in return for a home, all meals, fully paid health expenses, education and transport! - it comes at a price.

Horses in a natural herd situation will spend more than 50% of their time grazing, nearly 10% running or walking with the other 30-40% of their time standing, grooming, rolling, playing or lying down. Depriving them of these natural activities by locking them in a stable 23 hours a day, feeding them a diet of concentrated feeds and working them for one hour, often inappropriately, inevitably results in so called "behavioural problems", "stable vices" and/or "lack of performance".

On the other hand there are horses kept in paddocks without sufficient feed, shelter, care and attention who are also in a state of deprivation.

It is quite possible to find a balance and there are lots of happy, healthy horses performing to their optimum who enjoy the kind of life where their needs are catered for. They are thus able to provide their owners with the return they want:: pleasure, or top performance in their chosen sport.

This balance involves providing a good natural diet, shelter from the elements and pests, clean water, the opportunity to be part of a herd (even though they are not necessarily running together), room to self exercise, access to grazing (even if it is in the form of ad lib pasture hay) and thoughtful training. Keeping horses involves a lot of time and expense to which every horse owner will testify, but if a job is worth doing, it is worth doing well. If it is not possible to meet this responsibility it would probably be best to take up a less demanding pastime.

The modern horse (*Equus caballus*) proliferated in the wild for thousands of years by instinctively self medicating on a wide variety of herbs. At this time in history horse owners have an unparalleled opportunity to keep their animals healthy using the best of ancient wisdom and modern research.

The observer of horses grazing, even in hand, will be astonished by the care they take in selecting a variety of plants and special parts of those plants. Witness the horse carefully eating the purple flower heads off a scotch thistle avoiding the needle like thorns all around! In addition some horses will eat some plants while others will not, some horses will take one mouthful, others will eat as much of that plant as they can get at that particular time.

This book is devoted to providing practical information for the horse owner who wishes to keep their animals healthy in as natural and inexpensive a way as possible using herbs, Bach flower essences and natural feeds. It explains how to provide basic nutrition, preventive health care, performance optimisation and herbal medicine for the treatment of common ailments and diseases.

The information does not purport to take the place of specialist equine veterinary care and attention which is an integral part of responsible horse ownership and care.

2 THE HOLISTIC HORSE

HOW TO BEAT SWABBING

Undoubtedly this headline has grabbed the attention of every person who believes that there is such a thing as a magic elixir. A potion which will transform their problem horse into a dazzling winner in the twinkling of a wand. Alas the magic elixir does not exist - at least not in that context!

There is an answer.

It is called The Holistic Horse who has ...

          Physical Balance
          Mental Stability
          Perfect Nutrition
          Humane Training

These four things are the foundation stones which every thinking rider or trainer must give to their horses. In return they will receive success.

Sounds easy - but it means a lot of hard work, time, patience and brain power. The rewards, when the pieces of the jigsaw finally fall into place, make it all worthwhile.

THE SWABBING SYSTEM

There will always be those who will try to beat the system and often the horse is the one that pays which is most undesirable.

The system means abiding by the rules of competition, which in this context refers to refraining from using prohibited substances. These are considered to be performance enhancers, giving the user an unfair advantage.

A prohibited substance is any substance which has a molecular structure and can therefore be detected by swabbing, either through urine testing and/or blood sampling.

Drugs (and herbs) all have their own unique molecular structures, which can be likened to a finger print and can therefore be detected by swabbing.

Therefore it is the responsibility of any competitor to ascertain from competition organisers what that list is, in order to comply with the rules. It is just as much the responsibility of the organisers to make this list freely available and indeed to publicise it widely, so that competitors are given every opportunity to comply with the rules. Unfortunately it appears to be virtually impossible to obtain actual lists. Instead there is a vague "rule" which states that competitors must not administer anything to their horses which would enhance their performance.

I propose that there should be a national list which applies to each and every organisation running competitions under racing or equestrian rules so that there can be no misunderstandings. This list should be updated quarterly so that there is the opportunity for fair play on both sides of the fence. The rules should be designed to protect the best interests of the horse as well as preventing unfair advantages amongst competitors.

Rumours frequently abound to the effect that certain influential personalities escape justice. Unfortunately the average competitor is unlikely to be in a position to establish the truth or otherwise of these rumours but human nature being what it is, it is highly likely this does happen on occasions.

The flip side is that if you abide by the rules, you are protecting the best interests of your horses and your conscience will be clear.

HERBS AND SWABBING

At the time of writing there are a few herbs which appear on lists of prohibited substances - WHITE WILLOW, KOLA, KAVA, GUARANA and VALERIAN. However this does NOT mean that other herbs WILL NOT BE swabbed for.

White Willow contains salicylic acid which gives it anti-inflammatory and analgesic actions. Modern aspirin owes it origins to White Willow. Kava is a sedative. The properties of Kola and Guarana are similar to caffeine being heart stimulants, dangerous if over used and addictive.

These herbs provide a stark contrast to each other and highlight the importance of understanding that just because something is a natural substance it is not necessarily good.

It is also essential to realise that just because a small amount of a drug (or herb) is good, more is not necessarily better. The opposite is quite often true, which is why there are certain allowable very low levels of some drugs as part of swabbing rules.

With regard to Valerian - this appears to be in quite common use and in some cases at quite high dosage rates to obtain a sedative affect. Valerian is NOT the natural precursor to the drug Valium which is a popular misconception. It is a wonderful herb when prescribed correctly (useful in treatment of stringhalt and azoturia to name two conditions for which I may prescribe it). Even though it is classed as a nervine, that is a herb which influences the nervous system, generally speaking it is not going to be useful as a symptomatic sedative for the competition horse. Valerian is contra-indicated for horses which are predisposed to loose manure as a nervous reaction as it may make them worse.

THE BACH FLOWER ESSENCES

There is a class of natural substances which at this point in time cannot be detected by swabbing as they do not have a molecular structure. They are the Bach flower essences. These wonderful homeopathic style remedies are extremely useful in balancing horses and riders - especially the nervous ones, but they certainly  aren't going to make horses gallop faster, jump higher, turn quicker on their own.

It is my prediction that it will never be possible to detect Bach flower essences, nor will it be necessary, because they are designed to balance and harmonise holistically.

The appropriate and correct use of herbs is designed to do the same thing and therefore competitors who use herbs in this way have nothing to fear from returning positive swabs - unless they are using inappropriate herbs (either deliberately or through ignorance or bad advice) or over-dosing. The dosage rates I prescribe for my clients' horses are often less than some herbalists prescribe for humans ! I was trained to use drop dosages and these are very effective, IF the correct herbs are prescribed. In addition when the whole horse is balanced there is no need for further herbal treatment - the horse can be maintained on appropriate natural feeding which always includes some feed herbs such as Garlic, Linseed, Chamomile and Rosehips.

PHYSICAL BALANCE

The equine athlete must be physically capable of carrying out the tasks set for him. There are myriad reasons why performance can be impaired for a physical reason. There are a lot of obvious reasons and many more subtle. If one body system or part of one system is out of balance it will negatively influence other body systems. The most dramatic illustration is the musculo-skeletal system.

The orthodox view of unsoundness is that a horse shows actual lameness. This could not be further from the truth. Irregularities of pace, often accompanied by tilted polls, necks off to one side, faces making sideways or circular motions, agitated tail movements, shying, running away, becoming cross-gaited in canter and so on, are all manifested for a reason. It is up to the rider or trainer to ascertain and address the cause/s of these symptoms. These horses are anything from slightly uncomfortable to downright sore and the degree of pain they put up with depends on their personal pain threshold. Like many of the best athletes, sometimes the most successful and therefore the bravest horses are the ones that push through that threshold and become champions. Body therapies such as equine chiropractic and acupuncture carried out by veterinarians trained in these modalities and muscle therapies carried out by trained practitioners are of great benefit in this particular area.

MENTAL STABILITY

If a horse is not happy in his or her environment and circumstances, this will have a deleterious effect on performance. The thinking and experienced trainer will do their best to make sure their horses are content, but this may be to no avail. That same trainer will be able to recognise that a

particular horse is just not cut out to do what is being asked of it and a more suitable vocation is found.

Balancing the nervous system in the performance horse is a delicate business.

The intelligent use of prescribed, appropriate nervine herbs and Bach flower essences is an approach which often produces excellent results. In my experience, once the horse is balanced (usually takes one full blood cycle - 12 weeks), there should be no further need for treatment. In some exceptionally difficult cases it may be necessary for a horse to remain on treatment for longer than this or to be given a Bach flower mixture just on competition days. Horses should not remain on herbal treatments ad infinitum whether they are prescribed or proprietary mixtures. If it appears they need to remain on treatment the cause has not been addressed.

However, the environment, circumstances and training methods must also be taken into consideration and changes made where necessary.

PERFECT NUTRITION

One of the reasons horses escaped extinction some 6,000 years ago is that they were able to survive on a wide variety of plants and very poor quality roughage. Horses are no different now to what they were then. They are genetically engineered to do very well indeed on large amounts of roughage.

The problem now is that commercialisation has seen the proliferation of many artificial and unnatural feeds which have caused many problems for the horse. The same applies to other domestic species. The average horse owner cannot be blamed for succumbing to the power of advertising which tells them that these "complete", "fast", "cool" etc. feeds 'HAVE EVERYTHING IN IT'. But ask them WHAT is in it and they can't tell you.

"The advent of equine sports medicine in the past 50 years has not had any measurable influence on Thoroughbred speed records. They have remained virtually unchanged in that time." (2)

Excess feeding of salt, sugar, electrolytes, proteins, grains, un-natural feeds and synthetically manufactured minerals and vitamins unbalance the metabolism. This contributes to problems such as impaired immune function, scouring, gut ulceration, tying-up, arthritis and laminitis just to name a few.

"New diseases are constantly coming forward as man's rearing of domestic animals departs more and more from the natural." (3)

The cost of feeding horses natural feeds and supplements is much less than feeding commercial feeds, but it is slightly more time consuming.

The other advantage of feeding horses a natural diet is that the feeds can easily be customised. Horses like people have likes and dislikes. There are some feeds individuals do not tolerate or are better off without. The horse will tell you - it's up to us to work it out. Hence the old saying "The eye of the master fattens the beast."

HUMANE TRAINING

That great Australian horseman Tom Roberts, whose books are well know to many, always spoke about the importance of quiet persistence and teaching the horse to accept discipline by the "that will profit you not" method.

These same principles are embodied by some of the natural horsemanship methods now gaining popularity. They all require an understanding of how the horse thinks. Many people wrongly attribute human thinking ability to the horse.

Forceful training methods produce fear in the horse and are self defeating. Because of the phenomenal memory of the horse, that fear remains with him for life to some degree or other. These methods also create physical unsoundness, behavioural problems and impaired performance.

As the old saying goes "You can't make a silk purse out of a sow's ear". But you can do your best with the material you have to work with. The holistic horse principles provide that framework.

3 ARE YOU FEEDING AGAINST YOURSELF?

THE ADVANTAGES OF NATURAL FEEDS AND SUPPLEMENTS

Why do natural feeds and supplements produce a superior result compared with processed feeds, pellets, extruded feeds, "cool" feeds and pre-mixed fast feeds?

Consider this - how many of you prefer to sit down to a delicious home cooked meal or a cordon bleu dinner at a great restaurant rather than eat take-away, frozen food or tins every night? Now I know you wouldn't be a normal human being if you didn't enjoy the occasional binge on junk food - it's good for the soul - but EVERY NIGHT? Never.

The horse's genetic evolution has produced an extremely efficient machine that simply does not need or do well on the huge amounts of concentrated feeds, chemical supplements and injectable vitamins so widely used.

Feeding a selection of natural feeds and supplements to our horses - some of which have stood the test of time and others the result of modern research - has numerous benefits. The only small disadvantage is it takes longer to prepare feeds. Those horse owners who have chosen the natural way are so delighted with the results they never go back.

The benefits are numerous. The most significant is that natural feeding produces healthy horses with good disease resistance (prevention is cheaper and better than cure). It is more economical. It is easy to cater for individual needs. Quality and freshness control is easy. You know for sure what it is you are feeding, there is no hidden rubbish. There are no synthetically manufactured minerals and vitamins which are difficult for the body to metabolise. You can ensure you are not doubling up on ingredients which is wasteful, expensive, overloads the kidneys and liver and can in fact be deleterious to good health.

It is a well known fact that once the husk of the seed has been broken, the nutritional value is lost in a matter of days. Many prepared feeds contain rolled or cracked grains and/or cereals. Pellets can expand in the gut and the ingredients are usually no more than compressed pollard and bran or rice. Extruded feeds (often based on bran and pollard) are often old or worse stale by the time they reach the consumer, your horse.

Like fast foods for humans, fast feeds for horses contain added salt, sugar and other substances such as feeds unsuitable for horses, preservatives, colouring and emulsifying agents, humectants, flavour and palatability enhancers all of which can be damaging to the metabolism.

The famous animal herbalist Juliette de Bairacli Levy supports this view. *"... new diseases are constantly coming forward as man's rearing of domestic animals departs more and more from the natural." "Natural diet and herbal treatments, which are never destructive to the body tissues, are the simplest method of keeping disease from all livestock and curing those which are diseased..."*

This remarkable woman is a hands-on herbalist who has travelled all over the world treating animals and learning much from many different cultures of their approach to natural healing of their animals. While studying to become a veterinarian in the UK in the 1930s she became disenchanted with the influence which the huge drug companies were already having over treatment of disease. Her book which is quoted from here, *The Complete Herbal Handbook for Farm and Stable* is particularly valuable for its philosophy. It was first published in 1952 and has been reprinted ever since, the fourth edition being published in 1991.

A recent publication in many ways echoes some of her philosophy. *Complementary and Alternative Veterinary Medicine -* Schoen and Wynn (1998) emphasises the importance of preventive nutrition, the need to acknowledge biochemical individuality and the advantages of natural feed substances in equine nutrition. "Overall health and hair coat quality are consistently better when animals are fed live foods as opposed to processed foods."

The natural feeding programs outlined here are the foundation of a holistic program, designed to provide basic nutrition as well as preventive nutrition, that is to prevent disease by giving the body systems their best opportunity to remain in optimal condition.

When introducing a new feeding program do it gradually over a period of about 10 days, phasing out old feeds and introducing new ones a little at a time. Always keep the roughage content high.

CONDITIONING THE PERFORMANCE HORSE

There are many variables which affect the condition of horses and it is essential to consider these when working out amounts and types of rations. They are: size, age, breed, colour, occupation, current preparation goal, season, shelter, access to pasture/fodder quality, teeth, worming and individual feed conversion rate.

WEIGHING RATIONS

There is only one reliable and correct way to work out the amount of feed to give and that is to WEIGH IT. A set of kitchen scales is good for bran, grain and supplements while a weighing hook that hangs off the rafters in the feed room is ideal for weighing hay and chaff. A measuring jug is also essential for liquids.

Biscuits (slices) of hay tend to vary in weight a lot more than say grains and chaff, but they do all vary. So it's not much

good saying well I give him a dipper (scoop) of something, because everyone's dipper is different. You have to relate the volume to the weight.

Several dippers are handy: a chaff dipper that holds 3 litres (UK 5¼pt; US 6½pt) by volume which equals on average 750g (1lb 10oz) oaten or wheaten chaff or 1kg (2lb 3oz) lucerne chaff; a saucepan that holds 2 litres (UK 3½pt; US 4⅓pt) by volume which equals on average 1.5kg (3lb 5oz) whole oats or barley (corn is heavier) or 500g (1lb 2oz) bran; and an enamel mug (about the size of a large coffee mug) which holds 125g (4½oz) of black sunflower seeds.

With supplements, choose the scoop or spoon you are always going to use and check the weight on the kitchen scales. For example a tablespoon of seaweed meal weighs 12g (just under ½oz) and a tablespoon of dried Chamomile weighs only 2g.

SIZE

Quite obviously you are not going to feed a Shetland pony the same as a Clydesdale. Height, build, conformation, type and current condition must all be taken into consideration. An estimate of the horse's body weight is also helpful, which you can work out using a special tape measure available from most saddleries. The weight of an average sized horse is considered to be 400 - 450kg (880-990lb).

AGE

Young, growing horses and pregnant and lactating mares and serving stallions need more energy feed and protein than mature horses, even those in the highly demanding sports. Old retired horses also need special consideration.

BREED

Thoroughbreds can be difficult to condition especially ex-racehorses going into a new occupation as hacks or jumping horses. This introduces another dimension in the list of variables - horses which have been jammed full of steroids, antibiotics, synthetic minerals, vitamins, electrolytes and excess proteins whose systems are so unbalanced they just fall to pieces when they come off all of it cold turkey. They need spelling, good plain feeding and a herbal detoxification program. Ponies and many smaller crossbreeds and station horses are hardy types whose genetic background has given them the ability to "live on the smell of an oil rag", which is why they should never be overfed. The danger in this of course is laminitis. Seasonal grass founder is also common in ponies and smaller horses which highlights the expression "horses for courses" especially when it comes to feeding.

COLOUR

Dark coloured horses as well as those carrying black genes (including liver chestnuts) have a greater requirement for copper than lighter coloured horses. Many parts of Australia are deficient in copper and its natural partner cobalt. Details on how to safely supplement these two minerals appear elsewhere.

OCCUPATION

It is obvious that the energy requirements of a racehorse compared with a child's small pony for example are going to be very different. Or a pleasure horse compared with an eventer. The lowest energy requirement is for maintenance of current body condition (eg horse not in work in nicely covered body condition). The low range includes horses which are ridden lightly - say a few times a week. The medium range includes competition horses such as campdrafters, cutters and reiners, showjumpers, dressage horses and hacks. The high range includes racehorses, eventers, pacers and endurance horses.

There are also working horses - either on stations - or quite often weekend pleasure and even some competition horses that only get ridden once a week or occasionally. These work sessions can be quite rigorous so they need energy feed on work days.

SEASON/SHELTER

The time of the year and whether the horse is stabled and/or rugged is also going to have an effect on the amount of energy horses need to run themselves and/or to work. For example in the middle of winter in a cold climate, a horse, even if rugged, is going to have a greater need for energy feed than one which lives in a climate with mild winters and is stabled. More energy is needed in the winter to keep warm, particularly if they are not rugged and do not have access to shelter. Also some horses feel the cold more than others, while some may feel the heat and lose condition in a hot climate.

Horses who feel the cold may have suffered a chill in the past and can be improved by adding herbal teas to the feed which have warming qualities. Horses who really feel the heat may be suffering from a low grade chronic post-viral syndrome and can be balanced with a herbal blood detoxification treatment.

CURRENT PREPARATION GOAL

With performance horses it is very important to assess energy needs depending upon the stage of the preparation and the demands of competition. Coming back into work will require less energy compared with reaching peak fitness in a preparation regardless of sport. Grain rations should always be removed or dramatically decreased the night before a day off and on the day off, to avoid acid build-up, which can lead to tying-up. Herbal treatments are extremely effective in the prevention of tying-up in association with a suitable feeding program.

TEETH

If a horse's teeth are not attended to every 6 months by a reputable and experienced horse dentist it will not be able to chew the food adequately which will result in impaired digestion and a resultant loss of condition. In chronic cases this can lead to laminitis, scouring and/or infection and even life threatening conditions. Young horses should have their teeth first attended to prior to mouthing.

WORMING

Horses suffering from worm burdens will have impaired ability to hold condition and typically will have poor coat quality. Sound management practices together with routine feeding of fresh or dried granulated garlic and other herbal anthelmintics can reduce the incidence necessary for chemical worming. See section on herbal worming which also outlines management practices.

FEED CONVERSION RATES

Every horse is an individual, so that you have good doers and poor doers. For poor doers in particular it is important to ascertain the cause and treat them to rectify these problems, so that you are not throwing feed away on a horse that is not converting it well or you are starving a horse that is obese. Herbal treatments can be most effective in balancing metabolic rates and appetite in such horses.

PASTURE, HAY AND ROUGHAGE

When working out rations take into account the contribution access to pasture may or may not make. If it is minimal or non-existent, then you must provide plenty of roughage in the form of hays and chaffs. Good quality lucerne hay can be very high in protein (up to 23%), as can clover hay, which can also be very high in oestrogens. So to provide plenty of roughage seek out oaten hay, grass hay, clover hay or mixtures including lucerne, provided they are of good quality and well cured. Lucerne is a very good horse feed providing high amounts of calcium but, like anything, should not be fed in excess.

Clover hay especially red clover can be very high in oestrogens and care should be taken when feeding especially to breeding stock. It is a good idea to feed a mixture of hays and chaffs, one for provision of green feed where necessary and the other for provision of bulk roughage.

If horses have access to good pasture for part or all of the time, then the supplementary feeding requirement is much less, not just for roughage but for all feeds. Creating a balanced pasture especially for breeding stock is very important and expert assistance should be sought in this area. Unbalanced pastures can lead to all sorts of problems, one of the most notable being calcium deficiency caused by predominant grazing of African grasses such as Kikuyu. The oxalates contained in it inhibit the absorption of calcium and serious problems such as bighead and scouring can result. Soil analysis is recommended to discover the many likely mineral imbalances which can then be rectified using natural methods.

Horses are genetically designed to survive on large amounts of roughage and adequate provision of this is the first essential of basic nutrition. Depriving horses of enough roughage is literally starving them. See section on the digestive system and its problems.

CHAFF

Oaten chaff offers ideal bulk as the basis for mixing your own feeds. Depending on season and availability it may at times be necessary to feed lucerne chaff in addition to oaten chaff or instead of. It is a matter of balancing out the green and roughage in conjunction with hays and/or pasture. Excess wheat products should not be fed to horses which is why oaten chaff is preferable to wheaten chaff especially if you are feeding bran. However quality is always the prime consideration.

BRAN

An old fashioned feed currently out of favour in some circles, it is made from the outer layer of the wheat after the husk has been removed and is high in the mineral Phosphorous. It forms the basis along with wheat and rice pollard for many of the pelleted feeds on the market. Fed in excess it apparently interferes with the metabolism of Calcium in the body and should not be fed to horses prone to tying-up for this reason, nor should it be fed in excess at all. A good example of the rule that everything if taken in excess tips the balance from beneficial to non-beneficial. Very useful for making a small mash as a base for adding the natural supplements. Try to get "broad" or "racehorse" bran which is nice and coarse, which is very hard to get these days. Bran has always been considered as laxative but in fact is not and should be looked upon as part of the bulk ration. Rice bran is useful to feed to horses that are prone to tying-up but is only available from health food stores. Do not feed bran which looks like pollard. Wheat germ is an excellent alternative but is expensive.

POLLARD

Pollard is made from the inner layer of the wheat outside of the germ and whilst there is no doubt it does fatten horses, it should be avoided at all costs. It is the prime culprit in creating over acidity as well as impairing the wind through fatness on the inside. It is very fine and can impact in the gut and cause colic. Rice pollard is much higher in energy than wheat pollard and should also be avoided.

THE ENERGY FEEDS

These are high in carbohydrates (sugars and starches). The horse's body turns these into glucose (fuel) and glycogen (excess glucose stored in the muscle cells and liver for emergency uses). A constant supply of energy is essential for the competition horse. However excess can result in sore muscles, hot sore feet and fizzy behaviour.

OATS

Oats have the reputation of making horses "highly strung" but usually only do so if fed in excess, that is when the work load is insufficient compared with the amount being fed. But remember once again every horse is an individual and it is true that some horses do not tolerate oats well and they do create acid in these individuals. Oats are high in Phosphorous and useful to balance against the Calcium in the lucerne. Oats is an energy feed excellent for building healthy muscles and bones as it is also very high in Silica. Feed whole oats which you have freshly crushed or rolled yourself or which you have soaked in water for 8 hours first to soften the husk. Be careful this does not ferment in the hot weather - keep in a cool place or even in the fridge. Oats are an excellent energy ration for the young, growing horse and for all breeding stock.

BARLEY

Barley is more fattening than oats because of the higher energy value and does not make horses "hot" if fed properly. The best way to feed is to cook the whole grain gently just long enough to break the husk and take up the water. "Boiled" barley is a great conditioner without making the horse fat on the inside and outside like a horse which is fed pollard.

Some horses are oats horses and some are barley horses. Those which need muscle tone building and improved muscle bulk usually require oats and those which need an increase in body condition and maintenance usually require barley. If their occupation does not require much energy feed, they probably won't need either.

Feeding whole oats and/or barley in this way is very economical - the soaking, crushing or cooking makes the feed easier to digest for the horse so less is passed through undigested but does not destroy the goodness. Whole grains can be cracked or rolled if you have your own machine to do it, so long as they are fed within a few days so the nutrition value is not lost.

CORN

Corn is the highest in energy of the three (corn, barley, oats) and is very useful to feed to horses in demanding sports where high energy levels are required. Unless you are going to crack your own corn every few days, it is a good idea to feed corn as an oil. It is particularly useful to provide an important part of the energy ration for performance horses that are prone to tying-up. Start with 50ml daily for an average sized horse (450kg/990lb) and can go as high as 150ml daily depending on what other oils are being fed. Corn oil is high in linolenic acid which plays an important role in fat metabolism and therefore good digestion.

THE PROTEIN FEEDS

There is an absolute obsession with feeding huge amounts of protein these days and this is creating myriad problems.

BLACK SUNFLOWER SEEDS provide enough oil and protein for most horses when fed in moderate amounts. They are high in Vitamin E. The oil contains the Omega 6 essential fatty acids which have a number of benefits including inhibiting inflammation and activating immune cells.

SOYBEAN MEAL also provides oil and protein and is useful to give as well as the seeds where higher protein is required - mainly in breeding and growing horses. It also contains all the amino acids and the beneficial essential fatty acid - linolenic acid which are needed for digestion. Extra protein is needed when a horse is recovering from a debilitating injury or illness.

However soybean meal has been seen to produce hormonal behaviour in some horses. If this effect is seen, those individuals cannot tolerate soybean meal. Plain bred horses and ponies and good doers do not need soybean meal.

EXCESS FEEDING OF PROTEIN AND GRAIN

Most performance horses simply do not require the amount of protein and grains that they are fed. The need for protein does not increase with the amount of work. However protein is most important to the growing and breeding horse. Excess feeding of proteins to performance horses is expensive and creates problems which can easily be avoided instead of spending even more money on trying to combat the harmful effects. It is important to realise that all feeds contain protein, not just the feeds we know as protein feeds. Adult horses only require between 7% and 10% protein in their diet. However protein levels of 15% and higher are common! Horses have evolved to eat mainly roughage so the only reason for excess feeding of protein is ignorance and the effects of advertising. Many performance horses will receive enough protein from hay and grains. Lucerne can have as high a protein level as 23%.

Harmful effects of overfeeding of proteins and grains (carbohydrates) include both behavioural and soundness problems. Behavioural difficulties may include anxiety, tension, distraction, girthiness, behaving badly when ridden or floated (transported) and so on. Soundness problems include impaired liver and kidney function eventually leading to disease, poor hoof quality, heat in the feet which is a sub-laminitic condition, poor hair quality, inability to maintain condition, swollen legs (especially the hind legs), dehydration, early fatigue, thick urine often with excess ammonia, higher heart and respiratory rates, tying-up and gut ulceration.

FEEDS FOR PREVENTIVE NUTRITION

MILLET

Millet is very high in Silica one of the most important bone and nerve conduction minerals so it is very good to feed as a regular part of the diet especially to those horses who don't get oats. Must be cooked, soaked or crushed as for the other grains. French White Millet is the best type.

LINSEED

One of the absolute best feeds available as it contains high concentrations of the beneficial fatty acids, Linolenic Acid, Omega 3, and Linoleic Acid, Omega 6. Linseed is very good for the health of the digestive tract, ligaments and tendons, the immune system and prevention and treatment of arthritis. Be careful with amounts, especially with horses tending to loose manure, as Linseed has laxative properties. In areas where soils are sandy, it is useful to help remove sand from the gut and prevent it from accumulating. The safest and easiest way is to feed as an oil. Cold pressed linseed oil is recommended and can be fed at the basic rate of 25ml daily for an average sized horse. Raw linseeds should not be fed to horses without first boiling for at least one hour, as otherwise they are poisonous. Boiling linseed is difficult as it burns easily and boils over easily. Raw linseed oil and linseed meal have traditionally been fed to horses in small amounts, but this is not recommended as they become rancid easily. Cold pressed linseed oil is now available from specialist suppliers but is expensive compared with boiling raw linseeds. You can cook them together with the millet in a porridge which is easy and cheap - cover with double the amount of water and boil for an hour. Ratio of millet to linseeds is two to one.

OILS

Oils (fats) are important to keep coats healthy and shiny and are also useful as an energy source for horses who only have slow exercise. They also assist in the transport and absorption of fat soluble vitamins, minerals and protein.

Excess oil should not be fed to horses as they cannot easily metabolise excess as they do not have a gall bladder. However in moderation oils are most beneficial as noted above. Be sure not to feed oils which have become rancid. Oils must be stored out of direct sunlight.

Cod Liver Oil is well known as an arthritis preventative and will also assist in lessening the effects of arthritis in many cases - 10ml daily for all horses 10 years and over or those which have had an injuries especially involving trauma to bone.

Do not feed any oils or oil based feeds except those mentioned here. The others are usually of the variety which contain the non-beneficial fatty acids which promote the inflammatory response, pain and tissue swelling, or belong to the trans-fatty acid group and are genetically modified from industrial oils. They are therefore most undesirable as feeds for horses.

APPLE CIDER VINEGAR

Apple Cider Vinegar is a fabulous package and there are lots of varieties on the market for horses these days. Be sure to buy unpasteurised. The best is the locally grown organic variety. Apple Cider Vinegar is high in Potassium and also contains Phosphorous, Chlorine, Sulphur, Iron, Fluorine, Boron, Manganese, Silica and Magnesium. It is beneficial in the treatment and prevention of arthritis and being high in organic acids is useful in the prevention of viral attack. Apple Cider Vinegar is contra-indicated in some cases of scouring.

It is also a digestive aid and helps maintains the correct pH (acid/alkali balance) in the body.

Feeding Apple Cider Vinegar particularly for its Potassium together with Natural Rock Salt for Sodium and high grade Dolomite for Calcium and Magnesium provides electrolytes in a natural and easily metabolised form.

Depending on the size of the horse a daily dose of 20 to 40ml diluted in water and added to the feed is sufficient. This can be increased if circumstances warrant.

Apple Cider Vinegar also has many valuable external uses which are outlined in other chapters.

NATURAL ROCK SALT

All horses should have free access to lumps of natural rock salt which looks like pink quartz, for the provision of Sodium in a naturally occurring form. They take it as they require it thereby avoiding intake of excess salt, which upsets the electrolyte balance. Provision of Sodium and Potassium separately in a natural form is the easiest and best way to balance these two minerals. Feeding sodium chloride does not achieve the same result as the balance has been pre-determined and therefore does not take into account biochemical individuality.

GARLIC

Garlic is a fabulous package providing the minerals - Sulphur, Copper, Selenium, Chromium, Boron, Zinc and Molybdenum. Sulphur balances out the effects of heavy metals such as lead and cadmium and makes the blood less palatable to biting insects. Garlic is a natural vermifuge making the gut less attractive to worms attaching. Garlic is also a natural antibiotic with the huge advantage that it is selective, only destroying pathogens and leaving useful and friendly gut flora. Routine feeding of either fresh or dried, granulated garlic at the rate of 1 tablespoon daily for an average sized horse is recommended.

SEAWEED/KELP

It is very easy and economical to provide the majority of the minerals necessary for good health by feeding liquid kelp (preferably Australian) or seaweed meal. It contains Calcium, Sulphur, Zinc, Magnesium, Manganese, Copper, Iron, Iodine, Cobalt, Boron and Molybdenum and many other trace elements. There are hundreds of different seaweeds. The best is brown bull kelp or Bladderwrack, found in the very deep parts of the ocean. It contains 26% of mineral salts in organic form, meaning they are easily metabolised and alginates which are exceedingly high in protein. These mineral salts represent a vast array of common, rare and trace minerals and the highest plant source of Iodine, the critical mineral in thyroid balance. Australian seaweed products are recommended as they are harvested from non-polluted waters in the southern parts of Australia. Seaweed/kelp, like anything, must not be fed in excess. All the factors already discussed must always be taken into account when working out supplements. For seaweed meal, one heaped tablespoon (15g/½oz) daily is a guide for an average sized horse (450kg/990lb). For liquid kelp 10ml is the equivalent.

There are a few cautions and contra-indications on the feeding of Seaweed. Firstly ponies and plain cross-bred horses can just about "live on the smell of an oilrag" . They don't need too much of any feed, except adequate roughage. I come from the central western plains of Queensland and our horses lived and worked perfectly well on native grasses. Even offering ad lib seaweed to ponies is fraught with danger because a lot of them have ferocious appetites and will eat anything and everything that is available. Secondly there are those rare individuals who cannot tolerate seaweed - these horses are usually hyper-thyroid and therefore very sensitive to the Iodine in it. Other forms of mineral supplementation need to be worked out for these horses. Trouble commonly occurs when more than one mineral supplement is being fed at the one time.

DOLOMITE

Dolomite is a naturally occurring form of Calcium combined with Magnesium, one of its metabolic partners, which aids absorption in the gut. Feed only High Grade Dolomite which has a typical analysis - Calcium Carbonate 63% Magnesium Carbonate 35% Silica 2%. The base rate for feeding is one tablespoon daily for an average sized horse, but once again all factors must be considered.

Publicity claiming that minerals fed in the natural form are not as easily assimilated in horses' bodies as chelated or colloidal forms is a marketing ploy promoting these expensive forms of minerals. Horses are genetically engineered to ingest and absorb minerals in natural forms.

Why buy expensive synthetically manufactured minerals and vitamins when you can feed inexpensive and effective seaweed and dolomite?

MOLASSES/HONEY

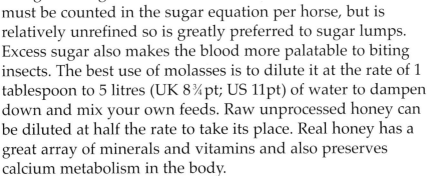

Molasses is often over-fed and is a major additive in sweet pre-mixed feeds. Excess sugar is contra-indicated for horses and is another cause of behavioural and soundness problems. The practice of feeding sugar lumps as regular treats can be enough to push a horse over the limit. Molasses even though it is high in minerals and vitamins must be counted in the sugar equation per horse, but is relatively unrefined so is greatly preferred to sugar lumps. Excess sugar also makes the blood more palatable to biting insects. The best use of molasses is to dilute it at the rate of 1 tablespoon to 5 litres (UK 8¾pt; US 11pt) of water to dampen down and mix your own feeds. Raw unprocessed honey can be diluted at half the rate to take its place. Real honey has a great array of minerals and vitamins and also preserves calcium metabolism in the body.

"Horses have a weakness for refined sugar which should not be indulged." " ...sugar lies within the province of "Yin" making it a negative element ... sugar takes energy from the body." " ...garlic lies within the province of Yang, that is, it is a powerful contributor of energy. The same applies to real honey ...." (5)

WATER

Water is an essential nutrient the importance of which is often overlooked. Lots of horses these days have to drink substandard water just like people, mains water which is high in chlorine, recycled water which often carries excess bacteria levels, river and irrigation channel water which may be polluted with various algae (like blue-green algae). Bore water not fit for human consumption must be analysed to see what the mineral composition is so that mineral supplementation may be adjusted in the feeding program. Bore water fit for human consumption is usually very good for horses, but once again the mineral composition should be checked.

Ad lib access to large quantities of clean, fresh water is the second principle of basic nutrition. Observing whether your horses are drinking sufficient water and taking steps to make sure they do if there is a problem is important. Water consumption is influenced by mineral content and contamination and horses may not consume enough water for balanced hydration in these situations. An averaged sized horse (450kg/990lb) needs to consume approximately 10% of its body weight daily in hot weather to maintain optimum water levels, that is 45 litres (UK 100pt; US 124pt). Generally speaking consumption will vary depending upon climate, temperature, age, size, work, electrolyte balance or if the horse is sick.

The three main and vital functions of water in the body are transport of nutrients and wastes, pH control and the dissipation of heat.

Also horses will often not drink enough water for reasons other than lack of cleanliness - automatic waterers and water from plastic buckets are two of the major culprits. Concrete troughs or enamel or stainless steel containers are preferable. Otherwise obtain best quality plastic. Test this by filling a container with water and leaving it in the sun all day. If it tastes of plastic at the end of the day, use it for manure instead.

Mains or town water can be made more palatable to horses and increase their consumption by the addition of high grade dolomite at the rate of one tablespoon to 45 litres (UK 100pt; US 124pt) and adjusted according to the size of the container. This will in particular take out the Fluoride and Chlorine. All water can be cleansed, particularly of harmful bacteria, by the addition of Colloidal Silver at the rate of one teaspoon to one litre of water. Charcoal filters and other commercial water filtering gadgets are also an option to consider.

4 THE MAGIC MINERALS AND VITAMINS

How do we know what minerals and vitamins our horses need? And how much? Why do we need to feed these supplements?

Scientific research stipulates very specific amounts of "average daily requirements". But one needs a good grasp of maths and lots of spare time to be able to work out how to arrive at this supposedly magical figure - for every mineral and vitamin! Equine research is limited in comparison with the human model and generally is carried out by the feed companies themselves, rather than by independent authorities. The result is that if you feed everything a company recommends, you find your weekly feed bill for one horse is quite simply far out of reach of the average horse owner. This is why I returned to natural feeding some 20 years ago. In addition many of the contents double up, the end result being that a lot of those expensive supplements are literally passed out onto the ground, overloading the horse's metabolism into the bargain.

The chemical degradation of soils resulting from the widespread use of water soluble fertilisers such as super phosphate, chemical pesticides and herbicides, has seen the depletion of many minerals from the feed chain. This is the basic reason for the necessity to feed mineral supplements.

Also the vast amounts of hormones, antibiotics, salt, sugar, stabilisers, preservatives and synthetically manufactured minerals and vitamins found in processed feeds means that they often lack nutritional value and can in fact be harmful.

Mineral patterns are inherited and arranged in a pattern from birth and are in a constant state of chemical equation throughout life. The full story on minerals and vitamins is not yet in. Research is constantly uncovering new information.

The big thing to remember is that most minerals interact with other minerals, each one needing others to be metabolised by the body. These interactions are complex and excesses of most minerals are often as deleterious as insufficient quantities.

The other essential piece of information is that minerals occurring in their natural form in raw food are very easily metabolised by the body and they usually occur in nature in balance with the other minerals, vitamins, enzymes, acids etc that they need to be metabolised. Any excesses will easily be excreted whereas the synthetic counterparts hold in the tissues, causing a range of health problems.

SYMPTOMS OF MINERAL DEFICIENCIES

Rough, dry, weak coloured coats, recurring disease patterns, wood chewing, dirt eating, tail eating are all symptoms of significant mineral deficiencies. Below par performance may often be the only apparent symptom of minor deficiencies. It is now widely recognised that minerals play a massive role in good health and simply preventing deficiencies is not enough.

Minerals, also known as elements, can be divided into three groups - those needed in larger quantities (macro), those needed in smaller quantities (micro) and those needed in minute quantities (trace) and are essential building blocks for vitality of life.

The important minerals for horses comprise CALCIUM, PHOSPHOROUS, SODIUM, POTASSIUM, IRON, MAGNESIUM, SILICA, SULPHUR, ZINC, COPPER, IODINE, SELENIUM, BORON, COBALT, MOLYBDENUM, MANGANESE, IODINE.

HOW TO FEED MINERALS NATURALLY

CALCIUM - The Bone Mineral
Calcium is essential for bone growth and
remodelling, digestion, metabolic rate, processing of
vitamins, acid-alkaline balance, stimulation of enzyme activity
and heart muscle health.Calcium and Phosphorous balance
each other and both are needed before either can react at all.
Good sources of calcium are green feeds, seaweed, molasses
and soybean meal. The highest source of Calcium found with
its metabolic partner Phosphorous is Chamomile. The cheapest
way to supplement Calcium is with high grade dolomite,
which is a naturally occurring form of Calcium with another of
its metabolic partners Magnesium. The best way is to also feed
flowers of Chamomile. An excess of Calcium will cause
Magnesium to be depleted and vice versa. Honey preserves
Calcium metabolism. Milk powder is not a good way to
provide Calcium as it is difficult to digest with insoluble
byproducts producing arthritic conditions.

PHOSPHOROUS - Balances Calcium
Phosphorous is essential for a healthy nervous system, for
processing of fats and carbohydrates, stimulation of enzyme
action and a healthy integumentary system (skin, hair and
hooves). Good natural feed sources are oats, bran, black
sunflower seeds, wheat germ, soybeans, millet, seaweed and
garlic. It interacts with Calcium as discussed above.

SODIUM - The Fluid Balancing Mineral
Sodium and Potassium work in harness, just as Calcium
and Phosphorous do. The ratio is essential for body-fluid
(hydration) balance, kidney health, pH balance and prevention
of arthritis. The kidneys are responsible for removing wastes
from the body via fluids so if there isn't enough sodium
dehydration will result and if there is too much there will be
fluid retention. Sodium in its natural form alkalises and is not

retained in body fluids while common salt (sodium chloride) produces an acid state with excess being retained in fluids. Chlorine combines with Sodium to act as a body and blood cleanser. Feeding common salt (sodium chloride) is certainly not the way to get these two valuable minerals into the horse's body. The best natural sources of Sodium are seaweed, celery, carrots and of course natural rock salt which can be bought in good feed stores in large or small lumps. It looks like pink quartz.

POTASSIUM - The Muscle Mineral

Potassium works in harness with Sodium to help regulate body fluid balance as discussed above. Potassium is essential for thorough elimination of wastes through the kidneys. It also regulates muscle function and tone. As the heart is a major muscle, this mineral is another important one for the equine athlete. Good feed sources are seaweed, bran, rice bran, wheat germ, black sunflower seeds and parsley. Apple cider vinegar is also a good source of Potassium.

IRON - The Fuel Mineral

Iron is the major fuel mineral and its role in the body is the transport of oxygen in the blood. Found in the red blood cells as haemoglobin it's action must be triggered by a trace of Copper without which it remains useless. It also needs Calcium present to ensure adequate absorption. Australia has iron rich but often copper deficient soils and more often than not supplementation with Copper is all that is needed. Natural sources of iron are seaweed, wheat bran, rice bran, oats, barley, soybean, parsley and dandelion. Excess Iron, combined with insufficient Copper promotes arthritic development.

MAGNESIUM - The Nerve Mineral
Magnesium needs a partner in Phosphorous
in order to react efficiently.
It regulates the nerve fibres that control the
central nervous system and helps to regulate
glandular function.
When muscular spasm occurs as in cramps or muscle soreness
from over-use or when muscles contract involuntarily under
stress, Magnesium is called for. The best way to get Magnesium
naturally is through high grade dolomite where it occurs
naturally with Calcium. Natural sources are seaweed, wheat
bran, wheat germ, dandelion, parsley, garlic and soybean.

SILICA - The Tough Mineral
Without Silica, Calcium cannot go about its
work of strengthening bones, hooves and
conditioning hair and skin. It also prevents
Calcium deposits around joints and breaks up
uric acid crystals around affected joints so is a major player in
the prevention and treatment of arthritis. The best way to get
Silica into horses is by feeding whole oats or millet. There are
many millet varieties and French White is the best. Apples are
also a good source of Silica.

SULPHUR - The Cleansing Mineral
Sulphur is a major blood cleanser and antiseptic
with beneficial effects on digestion and skin. Protection
from external and internal parasites can be promoted by
feeding Garlic which contains high quantities of
Sulphur and has a great package of other minerals with
their extra benefits. It also contains amino acids, needed
for protein metabolism.

ZINC - The Fertility Mineral
Zinc is needed for a healthy reproductive system in both
sexes. Good natural sources are seaweed, black sunflower

seeds and wheatgerm. Both the latter also contain Vitamin E, important for fertility, another of nature's clever little packages. Zinc has been found useful in healing skin problems. Excess Zinc depresses Copper availability.

COPPER - The Magic Mineral

Super phosphate completely inhibits Copper. A lot of Australian soils are deficient in Copper. These two facts means it is essential to supplement this mineral to ensure a healthy immune system, protection against internal parasites and resistance to disease, especially fungal diseases such as seedy toe, mud fever and ringworm. Anaemia is often the result of copper deficiency, rather than iron deficiency. Iron cannot be assimilated without copper. Australia has iron rich soils, so giving iron supplements is often not the way to remedy anaemia. Dark coloured horses, chestnuts, and especially liver chestnuts who carry the black gene, need more copper than lighter coloured horses. Seaweed is a good way to supplement Copper. Rosehips granules (Rosa Canina) are very high in Copper and this is a very good way to give extra copper safely, with many extra benefits. Other natural sources of Copper are garlic, parsley, dandelion and red clover.

SELENIUM

Another victim of artificial fertilisers, along with its metabolic partner sulphur. Like most trace minerals Selenium is equally dangerous in excess or deficiency. Extremely important for healthy muscles and fertility, especially of the stallion. Seaweed is the best natural source followed by Garlic.

BORON

Also deficient in Australian soils due to the unbalancing of soils caused by artificial fertilisers. Boron is needed for Calcium and Magnesium to be metabolised. If they are not arthritic conditions will inevitably develop. Creaking joints may be a symptom. Seaweed is the best natural source of boron, followed by garlic and apple cider vinegar.

COBALT

Cobalt deficiency is rare. Symptoms include subnormal temperature, lack of appetite, susceptibility to cold and unwillingness to move. Like Copper, Cobalt is needed for the health of red blood cells and if both are missing anaemia will be more serious. It triggers the synthesis of Vitamin B12 which is impaired when the body is under stress. Seaweed and rosehips are good sources of cobalt.

MOLYBDENUM

Only a trace of this mineral is needed for high fertility. Excess will inhibit metabolism of copper and cobalt which will lead to anaemia. Garlic is a good natural source.

MANGANESE

Important for healthy functioning of bone especially cartilage, nervous system, metabolism, nervous system and pH balance. Good sources are well grown green feeds, whole grains and apple cider vinegar.

IODINE - The Endocrine Mineral

Iodine is deficient in Australian soils. It is essential for the healthy functioning of the thyroid gland which is the conductor of all the other glands which make up the endocrine system. A deficiency can therefore be a basic cause of almost any problem. Obvious symptoms of deficiency include an enlarged goitre, scurf and/or grease. Seaweed provides sufficient Iodine. Excess feeding of goitragenic feeds such as soybeans, lupins, clover and lucerne is the main cause of iodine deficiency.

TRACE MINERALS

The role played by these minerals found in minute amounts in the body is not yet fully understood. Interestingly most of these are found in the glandular system. They include silver, aluminium, arsenic, tin, nickel and mercury. Colloidal silver was a useful and popular antibiotic in the 1930s and is currently undergoing a revival of interest and usage.

NATURAL v SYNTHETIC

Feeds containing natural, balanced compounds do not unbalance the body while those containing synthetic compounds do. This is true even if the synthetic compound has the same chemical formula. This is a compelling reason to provide horses with natural feeds and supplements. There is no scientific explanation for the difference. Possibly the answer is that it is impossible to improve on Mother Nature when it comes to feeding.

FREE CHOICE FEEDING OF MINERALS

Provided a horse is not too sick to sense their needs through instinct, one of the best ways to feed minerals is to offer them on a free choice basis. This can be done by offering naturally occurring forms of minerals plus separate natural salt blocks. If both are fed together, as in commercial licks, the salt may limit the mineral intake.

"If horses need minerals but not salt, they will not eat the mineralised block any more than a person would eat oversalted food. When horses are given plain minerals, the quantity they eat is often astounding (2 to 3 times normal intake) for a few months, until they have balanced out their minerals, then the amount consumed tapers off to a maintenance level." (4)

However this is often more applicable for paddock horses than stabled horses who can have suitable amounts included in the feed.

Mineral balance is more critical than vitamin balance for horses as a healthy horse will manufacture sufficient water soluble vitamins and receive sufficient fat soluble vitamins if properly fed.

VITAMINS FOR VITALITY

Horses that are stressed by ill health, toxins, viruses or heavy work and those with poor nutrition benefit most from vitamin supplementation. Harm can be done by overdosing. Do not fall into the trap of thinking that if a little is good more must be better, quite often the opposite is true.

There are two categories of vitamins - fat soluble and water soluble. Vitamins act as catalysts to the other nutrients. The fat soluble vitamins are A,D,E and K, which are absorbed, transported and stored in fats. The water soluble vitamins are Vitamin C and the large B group.

FAT SOLUBLE VITAMINS

VITAMIN A
Vitamin A is stored in the liver and fat tissue for use when needed. Found in green feeds, well cured hays, cod liver oil, carrots, dandelion, fenugreek and pumpkin. It is important for healthy vision, respiration, nervous system and reproduction.

VITAMIN D - THE SUNSHINE VITAMIN
Vitamin D is produced by the skin on exposure to sunlight and is also found in green feeds and sun cured hays. Essential for Calcium and Phosphorous utilisation in bone formation. If fed in excess as in the overuse of mineral/vitamin supplements it can cause calcium to be deposited in soft tissues such as heart, lungs and kidneys. Horses which are nearly always stabled and rugged should be given a few hours

in the sunlight every day as well as having enough hay and green feed.

Vitamins A and D are found in cod liver oil and fenugreek.

VITAMIN E
Vitamin E is important for cell division, in the prevention of muscle problems and prevents other vitamins from oxidisation. Good sources are well cured hays, oats, wheat germ, black sunflower seeds and parsley.

VITAMIN K
Vitamin K is necessary for normal blood clotting and is produced in more than adequate amounts in the horse's digestive tract. Also found in green feeds, bran, wheat germ and cod liver oil.

WATER SOLUBLE VITAMINS

The water soluble vitamins are the B group and Vitamin C which if fed in excess on a given day are lost in the urine, which means they need continual replacement. However in specific situations higher doses can be extremely useful, especially Vitamin C.

THE B GROUP

The Vitamin B Group also known as B Complex comprises the following - Vitamin B1 (Thiamine), Vitamin B2 (Riboflavin), Vitamin B6 (Pyridoxine), Vitamin B12 (Cyanocobalamin), Biotin, Inositol, Folic Acid, Pantothenic Acid and Choline.

Vitamin B1 (Thiamine) is often used as a supplement. It can be deficient where there is an upset in the lower bowel and the vitamin forming bacteria are disturbed, caused by illness, poor absorption or nutritional problems. Important for the health of the nervous and digestive systems. Natural sources are brewer's yeast, black sunflower seeds, wheat germ and rice bran.

Vitamin B2 (Riboflavin) is important in disease resistance when the body is under stress and for the health of eyes, lips and mouth. Natural sources are green feeds, brewer's yeast and wheat germ.

Vitamin B3 (Niacin) is important in the formation of enzymes and the balance of the adrenal gland. High natural sources are barley and brewer's yeast.

Vitamin B5 (Pantothenic Acid) is important in disease resistance, as it is needed by the body along with Vitamin C to manufacture its own cortisone. High natural sources are well grown green feeds, wheat germ and brewer's yeast.

Vitamin B6 (Pyridoxine) is important in resistance to infection and is of great value to the nervous system, appetite, digestion, red blood cells, blood vessels and liver. Good sources are green feeds, corn, brewer's yeast, wheat germ and soybean.

Vitamin B12 (Cyanocobalamin) is synthesised in the gut provided sufficient cobalt is present. Sickness, stress and use of antibiotics affects this synthesis and supplementation is very useful at these times. Lethargy and anaemia are two signs of Vitamin B12 deficiency. Natural sources are comfrey, red clover, echinacea, brewer's yeast and seaweed.

Biotin - an important vitamin for horses as it is necessary for hoof and hair growth. The best natural source is seaweed.

Inositol - a relatively new discovery thought to be useful in the elasticity of arteries and in the regulation of fat metabolism. Natural source is the same as many other B group vitamins - brewer's yeast and wheat germ.

Folic Acid - sometimes called Vitamin M - essential for conception. Good sources are green feeds The highest plant source is raspberry leaves.

Choline - important in liver function. Highest plant source is dandelion. Also found in brewer's yeast like the rest of the B group.

VITAMIN C - NEEDED AT TIMES OF STRESS

Vitamin C is manufactured by the horse but supplementation at times of mental and physical stress such as poisoning, vaccination, surgery and illness has proven benefits as demand then exceeds supply. Administration of drugs also interferes with the metabolism of Vitamin C and extra supplementation is also called for at these times. Vitamin C carries oxygen around the body in association with iron, binds cells together properly, assists in repair and renewal of cells (with Vitamin B12) and keeps blood vessels strong. The best plant sources of Vitamin C are rosehips (Rosa Canina) followed by parsley, dandelion and dock.

It is easy and relatively inexpensive to provide horses with all their mineral and vitamin requirements naturally. Many of the same feeds, herbs and natural substances feature under the listings for all the minerals and vitamins. And the bonus? Good disease resistance.

5 UNDERSTANDING HERBS FOR HORSES

Man has been using herbs to keep himself and his animals healthy for thousands of years. The earliest known records of herbal medicine may be traced back to the time of the Pharaohs in Egypt about 3000 B.C.

An interesting comparison with pharmaceutical medicine which has been around for less than a hundred years.

The wise words of ancient herbalists such as Hipprocates, Diascoredes, Galen, Culpepper and Gerard, to name a few, are still referred to today. Modern findings have added to this huge body of knowledge. Therefore it is quite possible to become confused about the diverse applications of many individual herbs.

As in human health there is an ever increasing trend towards the use of herbal medicine for horses and other animals. Owners are looking for viable alternatives to drugs, surgery and euthanasia. As a result there is a proliferation of "natural" and "herbal" products on the market. A quick check on the label may often reveal a minimal amount of natural substances and herbs in these products. This adds to the confusion.

FORMS OF USING HERBS

For culinary herbs, fresh is best, but it's certainly seldom the case for medicinal purposes. Practically speaking it's impossible. Also it is essential to be sure that you are using the correct plant.

Dried herbs added to the feed is a good way of feeding herbs to horses as part of basic nutrition and preventive health nutrition. Making teas from the dried herbs and adding the whole lot including the dregs is more time consuming but increases the potency.

Infusions (also known as teas) can be made from fresh or dried herbs which are soft, such as flowers and leaves. They are usually made by pouring 600ml (21fl oz) of boiling water onto 30g (1oz) of herb and allow to infuse for 15 minutes. You can put the dregs of the herb used to make the tea in the feed as well. If you want to give a herbal tea quickly as medicine, strain it once it is cool and then use it as a drench.

To use hard plant material such as seeds, roots, bark, etc., a decoction is made by pouring 750ml (26fl oz) cold water over 30g (1oz) of the cut up material in a saucepan and setting aside for 12 hours. Bring to boil and simmer for about 20 minutes so that water is reduced to 600ml (21fl oz). Strain before using or storing in the fridge for a couple of days. Infusions (teas) or decoctions extract the medicinal qualities from the herbs.

The shelf life of dried herbs is only 3-6 months from the date of harvesting. They are best stored in brown paper, cellophane or glass, NOT in plastic containers. Certified organically grown herbs, especially those grown in Oz, are highly recommended for their superior quality. Increasing amounts of these are becoming available direct from growers and from reputable suppliers.

For medicinal purposes, trained herbalists prescribe extracts and tinctures which are made from herbs using alcohol to extract the medicinal qualities and to act as a preservative. Well made extracts and tinctures have a shelf life of 2-3 years when stored in brown bottles away from sunlight and below 30°C (86°F). Very small dosages are most effective and easy to administer by syringing over horses' tongues mixed with an equal amount of water. A common dosage I use is 4ml twice daily containing a mixture of five herbs and five Bach flower essences. Most horses quickly learn to relish herbs given in this way. My horses open their mouths for their herbs with no halters on and many of my clients report the same response. Alternative methods of dosing include offering the

herbs as part of a very small amount of feed or water. A major advantage of using herbal extracts as medicine is the non-invasive nature of dosing compared with injections.

EXTERNAL USES

Herbal oils, ointments and washes are extremely effective and useful for external use especially for first aid. Five essential ointments for the first aid kit are - Arnica for bruising (if the skin is not broken), Witch Hazel for bruising (if the skin is broken), Thuja for greasy heel and other fungal complaints, Calendula for wounds, cuts and abrasions being antiseptic and soothing and Comfrey for healing, but only if there is no infection present.

You can obtain these ointments from specialist suppliers, health food stores or make them yourself. If buying these from health food stores, check carefully to make sure there are no added ingredients as these can sometimes be contra-indicated from the simple effective use of these ointments.

OILS

Comfrey Oil is absolutely superb for hastening hoof growth, improving hoof quality, repairing grass, sand and quarter cracks. It is also very useful for healing lumps and bumps on legs and applying to strained and sprained tendons and ligaments. For the latter it is worth adding raw linseed oil as well in equal parts to help restore elasticity. Comfrey Oil can be made by using 4 parts olive oil to 1 part ground Comfrey root and leaving in the sun in an airtight clear jar for 2 weeks, shaking occasionally. Strain into a brown glass bottle for storage and application.

Hypericum Oil is excellent for soothing bites, itchiness and allergic reaction on the skin even where odoema is present as a result and also for larger areas of skin affected by hair loss, including rubbed manes and tails. It can be made in the same way as the Comfrey Oil but the flowers of Hypericum are the part of the herb to use.

To prevent flies, mosquitoes etc. from biting make up an insect repellent which can be sprayed on or sloshed on with a sponge taking care to avoid the eyes. To a 500ml (17½ fl oz) spray pack add half water and half apple cider vinegar, 15 drops Oil of Citronella and 5 drops Oil of Pennyroyal. To make this more potent and to deter ticks as well replace the water with strained Wormwood tea and add 5 drops of Eucalyptus Oil. Use a good handful of the dried herb to a litre of water.

POULTICES

A green leaf poultice is one time when fresh herbs are best

employed. Comfrey leaves are ideal for making a poultice to treat sprains, strains and other injuries. Pulp the leaves with some water, spread on a piece of gamgee and bandage onto legs to relieve bruising, inflammation, sprains, strains, shinsoreness and to promote healing. Or you can keep a quantity of dried and minced comfrey leaves on hand for this purpose. Make up and apply a fresh poultice daily, especially if the skin is broken.

Poultices can be helpful in drawing infection out as with puncture wound and abscesses. For these use castor oil or raw honey and Slippery Elm Bark Powder made into a paste. If using castor oil make sure there is a hole in the tissue to draw the infected material out. If not use raw honey instead.

WASHES

Herbal washes are made by diluting herbal extracts in water for various uses.

To make an antiseptic cleaning wash for the sheaths of stallions and geldings, a mixture of equal parts of Hypericum and Calendula extracts with the Bach flower Crab Apple is diluted at the rate of 10ml to a litre (35fl oz) of water.

For healing sores caused by allergies, such as the one from ergot in Paspalum grass, use a mixture of Golden Seal and Calendula extracts with the Bach flowers Crab Apple and Rescue Remedy diluted at the rate of 20 drops to a teacup (250ml/8½fl oz). This wash, at an increased rate of 30 drops to a teacup, is also suitable for the treatment of contagious skin conditions such as ringworm together with internal treatment. Practical measures to prevent other horses (or people) from becoming infected must also be taken. This means disinfecting rugs, tack and grooming gear and isolating the horse. People handling the infected horse must wash their hands thoroughly with soap and water every time before they touch anything else.

For bathing and soothing sore or inflamed eyes, the same

mixture diluted at the rate of 10 drops to a teacup can be used. Great care must be taken to ensure the dilution is correct, use a fresh cotton wool swab every time and for each eye. If you suspect the eye may be injured, and the horse is in pain, immediately put the horse away from direct sunlight and call an experienced equine vet to examine the eye BEFORE doing anything else.

To stop bleeding apply a mixture of Yarrow and Calendula extracts with the Bach flower Rescue Remedy straight together with physical pressure. To disinfect wounds and to continue to prevent infection use 20% Calendula extract in water daily. A tea can also be made from dried Calendula flowers, strained and cooled to use for the same purpose.

WHICH HERBS TO USE?

Herbs are well employed in several different ways - as part of a natural feeding program to provide basic and preventive nutrition and therapeutically as medicine to treat body imbalances and diseases.

It is relatively straightforward to recommend herbs to form part of a natural feeding program to provide basic and preventive nutrition. This has been covered in previous chapters. But herbs to be used as medicine should be individually prescribed for each horse taking into account all the relevant factors - physical, personality, circumstances, health record, diet, any veterinary diagnosis etc. To prescribe successfully one needs herbal medicine training and considerable hands-on experience of horses as a rider, trainer and stable manager.

These are the main reasons why I do not believe that many proprietary herbal mixtures are effective. There are herbs in the mixture which are not applicable to the horse in question or may even be contra-indicated, usually the quantities of each particular herb are too low, shelf life of dried mixtures has a definite question mark, and the cost is high. And there is no recommended course of treatment. To my way of thinking quite often there are herbs included in these mixtures which simply do not relate to the claims on the label.

To feed herbs for basic and preventive nutrition it is much cheaper and more effective to select good quality dried herbs from a reputable supplier. That way you can also buy in bulk at a discount.

HOW HERBS WORK IN THE BODY

Drugs can quite often produce undesirable side effects. Whilst herbs like other medicines do have cautions and contra-indications, provided these are followed, appropriate herbal treatments with suitable dosage levels very rarely have unpleasant side effects.

Major additional benefits are the synergistic action of herbs and the absence of risk from accumulation of waste products as occurs with chemical medicines. The constituents of herbs such as minerals often occur with their natural metabolic partners - other minerals or vitamins along with other substances such as tannins, glycosides, tissue salts, enzymes and so on which synchronises the action of the whole plant. Please note that medicinal plants are species only, not cultivars which have been hybridised or otherwise genetically modified. So there is no point in rushing out and picking bits off some of the plants you might have growing in the garden such as marigolds or rosehips for example to use medicinally!

SYNERGY

An excellent example of synergistic action of a herb is provided by Meadowsweet. "It is the herbal aspirin - but better, and without any of the side-effects! Meadowsweet contains a substance called salicylic acid which is found in the flower buds; the same substance is also found in the bark of the willow - Salix alba. In the late 1890s the pharmaceutical company Bayer formulated a new drug called acetylsalicylic acid, which we know better as aspirin. It is the salicylates in meadowsweet that have the anti-inflammatory action on rheumatic pain and fever, as well as being antiseptic and diuretic. They are balanced by the other constituents in the plant, such as the tannins and mucilage. The salicylates in isolation can cause gastric bleeding - a now well-known possible side-effect of aspirin. However when the plant is left whole, in balance with its other constituents, then you have the opposite effect - a herb which is actually used to heal gastric bleeding and ulceration! Thus meadowsweet is an excellent example of the whole being better than its isolated components, and an example of how, when man interferes with nature he creates imbalance." (8)

Waste products are passed out of the body quickly and easily which is not the case with synthetically produced chemical medicines. Complete elimination of wastes is the key to real health. Arthritis is a very good example of a disease which can easily be prevented with the use of natural feeds and herbs ensuring healthy functioning of liver, kidneys and the other organs of elimination.

CLASSES OF HERBS
AND THEIR ACTIONS IN THE BODY

These include alteratives, anodynes, anti-spasmodics, antiseptics, astringents, demulcents and emollients, rubefacients, diuretics and diaphoretics, nervines, vulneraries, bitters, carminatives, vermicides and vermifuges.

ALTERATIVES

Alteratives are given in small doses for a full blood cycle (12 weeks) to cleanse the blood of the remains of an earlier infection that has not been completely removed (chronic) or in larger quantities over a shorter period of time for current infection (acute). Their action in the body usually causes elimination of some kind - for example loose manure, increased urination, coughing, sweating. As the horse gradually feels better and better, expect a glowing coat, balanced energy levels, improved body condition and general vitality. Alteratives are especially useful in the treatment of viruses affecting the respiratory system (such as EHV4) or the joints, post-viral syndrome and in the healing of stubborn infections anywhere in the body which have not responded to antibiotics. Alterative herbs include Garlic, Red Clover, Echinacea, Horsetail, Dandelion, Celery, Burdock and Agrimony.

NERVINES

Nervines as the name implies affect the nervous system. In herbal medicine for horses they are as important as alteratives, the two together producing significant improvements in overall health and therefore performance. Nervines work by balancing the nervous system, so that energy is expended when required and relaxation follows easily. Most owners of nervous horses who use up their energy BEFORE they are called to and are then exhausted or unable to perform to optimum will identify with this statement. Nervines lessen symptoms and correct causes at the same time. Once the nervous system is balanced there is usually no further need to administer nervine herbs. Occasionally a really difficult horse that has taken much longer than usual to balance may require maintenance treatment, but even those usually end up being maintained on an individualised natural diet. The nervine herbs used for horses are Chamomile, Hops, Valerian, Vervain, Skullcap, Mugwort and Passiflora.

ANODYNES, ANTI-SPASMODICS, SEDATIVES, ANTI-INFLAMMATORIES

Pain is nature's way of telling a body to rest so that healing can take place. Herbs are used in conjunction with spelling for reducing the intensity of pain but they do not block pain in the way that drugs do. They can be used for relatively long periods of time as they also have healing properties.
The underlying causes are differentiated to select the most appropriate herb. Anodynes reduce the intensity of pain. Anti-spasmodics reduce pain by releasing spasms in muscles and organs, returning blood flow and normal nerve signals to the area. Sedatives calm over-excited nerve signals which manifests as a type of pain or discomfort to the over reactive horse. Anti-inflammatories are used to reduce heat and swelling usually occurring in localised areas such as the legs. Herbs in this group include Meadowsweet, Black Cohosh, Hops, Chamomile, Valerian and Devil's Claw.

ANTISEPTICS

Herbal antiseptics are used internally and externally, often concurrently with alteratives. They are selective in their action, destroying the ability of pathogens to reproduce thereby keeping them at a manageable level, promoting an immune response and leaving friendly organisms to get on with their job of scavenging. Antiseptics reduce the likelihood of abnormal population imbalances. It is a physical impossibility to kill all germs - despite what TV advertising tells us. Antiseptic herbs include - for systemic use internally - Garlic and Echinacea, for external use Calendula and Golden Seal and internally specifically for urinary tract infections - Uva Ursi, Cornsilk (for mares) and Clivers (for geldings and stallions).

ASTRINGENTS, DEMULCENTS, EMOLLIENTS

Astringents re-establish fluid balance in tissues so that fluid loss and fluid retention are equalised. They are used internally and externally to re-arrange fluids including blood. Yarrow is a brilliant styptic when used externally to stop bleeding, especially in conjunction with pressure and is used internally for diarrhoea. Witch Hazel is only ever used externally for any type of oedema including filled legs, big knees and capped hocks.

Demulcents and emollients comfort and soothe internally and externally respectively. Herbs with a high mucillage content have this action forming a protective layer which promotes healing by reducing inflammation, irritation, pain and discomfort. Demulcent herbs are used to heal gut ulceration for example and include Marshmallow and Slippery Elm Bark Powder. Emollients include Aloes which can also be used internally.

RUBEFACIENTS AND CARMINATIVES

Rubefacients are used externally to stimulate and increase blood supply to an area. Care must be taken in their use as they literally cause redness and irritation and must be kept away from eyes, mouth etc. Excessive use can cause blistering. Wintergreen is a very good example of a rubefacient which when added to other oils is useful for treating muscular problems and also carries the beneficial effects of the other oils deep into tissue, including hooves.

Carminatives have the same warming and stimulating affect - internally. They reduce flatulence, improve digestion and soothe the digestive tract. They are also very useful for horses that have caught a chill or who feel the cold. Herbal teas in the feed are an easy way to give them - Parsley root, Celery seeds and Peppermint being three of the best. For a quicker result, cool and strain the tea and use as a drench. Do not think that carminative means to make calm. Herbs that have a calming or sedative affect are called calmatives.

DIURETICS AND DIAPHORETICS

Both of these classes of herbs work on fluid excretion processes, very important indeed in the performance horse. Diuretics work internally stimulating kidneys to produce normal urine excretion while diaphoretics work on the skin to stimulate sweating. Diuretic herbs are very useful for horses that are not getting rid of waste products (such as lactic acid) efficiently enough and in balancing hydration in horses that do not drink enough especially when they are out at competitions. Celery and Juniper are the big two diuretic herbs. Diaphoretic herbs are always part of a mixture to treat anhydrosis and include Fenugreek, Capsicum and Elder Flowers.

VULNERARIES, STYPTICS

Vulneraries are used to resolve bruising which usually affects the veins and often the lymphatics as well. The quicker vulneraries can be applied externally the better - Arnica ointment if the skin is not broken and Witch Hazel ointment or lotion if the skin is broken. Styptic herbs, Yarrow being the most famous, are more strongly astringent and are needed to help stop bleeding from arteries together with physical pressure. Antiseptic herbs such as Calendula should be used in conjunction whenever the skin is broken.

VERMICIDES AND VERMIFUGES

Vermicides kill worms in the gut, or elsewhere, and vermifuges expel the dead parasites and any associated debris from the body. This class of herbs are all strongly bitter and therefore distasteful to worms. The high tannin content and astringency cause contractions of intestinal mucosa. The herbs in this class are Aloes, Rue, Tansy, Wormwood, Garlic and Male Fern. The latter is difficult to obtain these days. The main disadvantage is that Aloes, Rue and Wormwood are contra-indicated for use in pregnant mares because of the stimulation of internal muscles, which could cause contractions. However Garlic is safe to use in pregnant mares but should be discontinued a month before and after foaling as it will taint the milk. See Herbal Worming.

Herbs usually have more than several classes of action in the body - often complimentary. In the List of Useful Herbs the major classes of action are all included. "The Big Six" Portmanteau Herbs - Garlic, Dandelion, Rosehips, Comfrey, Yarrow and Chamomile are of particular interest.

6 FIRST AID
HERBAL AND PRACTICAL

A good knowledge of practical and herbal first aid is the best insurance any horse owner can have.... it can help you decide quickly whether you need to call the vet or not. There are many useful measures you can take while waiting for the vet and in less serious cases, you can treat the problem quite adequately yourself. *Especially useful for all those people who live a long way from the nearest vet.* Fast and appropriate first aid usually prevents complications from setting in and usually results in faster and more complete healing.

READING THE VITAL SIGNS

One of the first procedures you need to learn (or perhaps brush up on) is how to read the vital signs. These are ...

RESTING HEART RATE

TEMPERATURE

RESPIRATION RATE

GUT SOUNDS

GUM COLOUR

LYMPHATIC CHECK

For this you will need a stethoscope, a thermometer, a stop watch and an observant attitude. It is a good idea to know the individual resting heart rate of your horses which you can work out by listening with your stethoscope to the heart (against the chest just behind left elbow) and counting for a period of 60 seconds when they have been at rest.

The normal rate is 40 beats per minute but many horses are lower.

The new thermometers are extremely simple to use - normal temperature is 37.5°C (99.5°F) - give or take a little for the time of day and the ambient temperature. Insert in the anus for 30 seconds making sure the thermometer is registering zero beforehand.

To work out the respiration rate - watch the flank or the nostrils and count how many breaths per minute. Do this a few times to compare in the healthy horse. Normal respiration rate is 10-14 breaths per minute. The rhythm is important. In the normal resting horse inspiration and expiration are followed by a pause.

Gut sounds can be checked by listening at the hollow just in front of the hip bone on the off side, with or without a stethoscope. This is the site of the ileo-caecal valve (between small and large intestines) and this should discharge approximately once very 60 seconds. Normally this is a very distinct noise from the other gut sounds. As one of my revered vets once put it "sounds like farting in the bath"! Over-active or under-active gut sounds can both be signs of trouble. The absence of the noise of the ileo-caecal valve discharging can indicate impaction colic. So get to know what your horses' normal gut sounds are like to avoid panic.

Checking gum colour and holding your thumb on a spot for a few seconds to see how quickly the capillaries refill is also a good test to see if circulation is normal. Gum colour should be pink, not very pale or too red or mauve or whitish-grey.

Also be observant for any enlargement in the lymph glands - around the base of the jaw and going around the jaw bone to under the ear is the place to check.

VIRUSES

If a horse appears lethargic and/or is off his feed and has an elevated heart rate, temperature and/or respiration rate, this is serious, as he is most likely coming down with a viral infection. Good nursing is of the utmost importance in caring for horses suffering from viral attack and prevention is better than cure. Horses suspected of being under viral attack must be must be protected from temperature variations as much as possible, must be rested and not subjected to stress of any kind. Viruses and post-viral syndrome can be prevented and treated effectively with prescribed herbal medicine. Routine feeding of garlic, rosehips tea and organic apple cider vinegar are especially helpful in prevention as well as treatment. Viruses commonly affect the respiratory system or the joints.

COUGHS AND COLDS

To relieve symptoms of a dry cough, add 2-3 drops of Oil of Eucalyptus to water or molasses water used to dampen down the feed. Do not add more than this or you will risk burning the mucous membranes and causing distress.

If the horse is coughing with a cold and has an abnormal nasal discharge double the routine dose of Garlic and Rosehips. Lemon is a wonderful and readily available antiseptic. Add the juice of a lemon and a tablespoon of honey dissolved in water used to dampen down the feed.
A tablespoon of dried Thyme leaves can be brewed into a tea and added as well for their soothing and expectorant action.
Be sure to keep the horse warm and out of the wind.

COLIC

Colic can be life threatening or a mild attack may pass unnoticed with no problem.

Symptoms include obvious discomfort, sweating, looking around at the gut, pawing, rolling and inability to pass faeces or frequently passing faeces. If colic is suspected immediately administer Rescue Remedy and lead the horse continuously so that it cannot lie down or roll and immediately call your vet. Also syringe 60ml strained and cooled Chamomile Tea for its anti-spasmodic effect. Repeat the Rescue Remedy and Chamomile every half hour. Mild cases will usually respond quite quickly. A fresh green pick is often appealing and helpful for these horses as well.

Routine feeding of Chamomile Tea is useful for the horse that is prone to colic as it is soothing to the gut and promotes good digestion. Causes of colic are numerous but can include ingestion of sand, inappropriate feeding (insufficient roughage in particular), worm burdens or something like a horse gorging large quantities of feed or getting a big gutful of cold water after being hot. Causes are often unknown but if the cause is known or suspected, this is helpful for your vet to know. There are different types of colic (impaction and spasmodic) and it is imperative it is treated by a vet who is able to differentiate and will decide on the most appropriate treatment.

This is one time when the quick action of veterinary prescribed drugs is really useful. However herbal treatment is helpful for horses who have suffered a serious colic attack and need help in full recovery, especially those horses which have had an operation.

INJURIES

These range from minor cuts and abrasions to a more serious injury which requires veterinary attention including stitching. The first thing to do is to STOP THE BLEEDING. This can be done using a towel or similar with pressure on the wound and concurrently apply a styptic to help staunch the flow. Yarrow is the herb which is particularly useful for this - a handful of fresh leaves will do or better still apply a mixture of Calendula and Yarrow herbal extract (straight if you are really in a hurry) or diluted at about 15% extract in water. Calendula is added for its highly antiseptic properties. Once the bleeding has stopped it is possible to assess whether you can care for the wound yourself or whether it needs veterinary attention. Administer Rescue Remedy internally. For minor wounds you are going to care for yourself - after stopping the bleeding, clean the wound by flushing with a mild saline solution in a syringe. Follow up with diluted Yarrow and Calendula extract and then bandage if necessary. Ensure Tetanus injections are given if they are not up to date. For the first three days AT THE VERY LEAST the most important thing to do is to prevent infection. Regular cleaning (as above) and applications of Calendula either 15% extract diluted in water or ointment form is recommended. Calendula is also helpful in preventing scarring. Apply raw honey as well with or without a bandage.

Once you are very sure there is no risk of infection, you can assist healing with the use of Comfrey ointment or a poultice of fresh Comfrey leaves pounded with water and held in place with a bandage. Dried Comfrey leaves can be kept on hand to reconstitute as a green leaf poultice using water. Castor oil is useful for floating debris out of puncture wounds and later on is good for helping grow hair back. Comfrey also plays an important role in the prevention of arthritis developing at a later date which is always a risk with injuries.

HONEY

My farrier, Sandy Parker, tells a marvellous story graphically illustrating the healing power of honey. He was up in the Northern Territory of Australia and one of the black stockmen had a horse with an extensively but freshly wounded shoulder. The man went over to a small papery bark type of tree, stripped some bark off to reveal bush honey underneath. He then applied the honey to the wound with the soft bark on top and bandaged it on. Sandy did not think the horse would survive. A few months later he was back at the same station and coincidentally saw the horse - completely healed and sound, with very little scar tissue!!!

Honey can be used internally and externally as a powerful natural antibiotic and healer. There is only one thing to remember - only use raw, unprocessed, unpasteurised honey which you can get from your local beekeeper or health food store. Do not use the supermarket variety as it will not work having been stripped of its healing powers by the processing. Some varieties of honey are more effective than others, the most famous being Manuka (New Zealand), Jelly Bush (Australia) and White Heather (Scotland). However all raw honeys are suitable to use for healing purposes.

UNDERSTANDING HEALING

"A clean wound will begin the process of healing immediately after the injury. Wounds that require stitching should be stitched as soon as possible after the injury so that the edges can be brought into direct contact with each other and must be clean. This is known as healing by primary intention. If the wound cannot heal this way, it must undergo the process of granulation, contraction and epithelial cell multiplication and migration. This is called healing by second intention. The formation of excessive granulation tissue (proud flesh) in wounds to the limbs also interferes with healing, as the epithelial cells cannot migrate over the proud flesh to create a new skin covering. If scarring occurs over or near a joint, the skin may be pulled so tight as to prevent proper joint movement." (6) The formation of excessive proud flesh can usually be prevented and treated with the use of raw honey with Calendula and Comfrey ointment.

BRUISING

If bruising is present either locally or systemically homeopathic Arnica 6 C should be given orally - 1ml hourly for the first 3 hours, then 3 times daily. For longer term usage twice daily is sufficient. Immediate application of ice packs, ice boots and/or cold hosing is most important for localised bruising. Pressure bandages under padding may also be called for provided you have the knowledge to apply these correctly.

If there is bruising without a break in the skin immediately apply Arnica ointment and maintain for a few days depending upon the severity. This will heal the bruising at a very quick rate and can also be used on stone bruises. For severe cases or cases where there is systemic bruising (such as in the case of a fall) homeopathic Arnica 6C used internally is also indicated. DO NOT USE Arnica topically if the skin is broken.

If there is bruising and the skin is broken use Witch Hazel ointment which will have the same effect with Calendula ointment (to prevent infection) or the two mixed together. Witch Hazel extract is also good in cases of big knees and capped hocks to draw the fluid back into the tissues.
The sooner this is used the better it will work.

LEGS - SPRAINS AND STRAINS

A solution made with Witch Hazel extract is good for legs which are slightly filled due to extra stress caused from bad ground or more work than usual. Apply after cold hosing and then leave or apply stable bandages. If a sprain or strain is obvious, follow directions under bruising and injuries. Internally administer Devil's Claw extract for its anti-inflammatory, analgesic and healing affects. From 2-10ml 2-3 times daily (mixed with an equal amount of water) depending upon the severity of the damage, for a few days.

Quick resolution of bruising and complete healing of injuries using herbs internally and externally together with appropriate diet is your best bet to prevent these areas from becoming a site for osteo-arthritic degeneration later in life. Prevention is better than cure - especially for this debilitating condition.

EYE INJURIES

When an eye injury is suspected the first thing to do is to protect the horse's eye from sunlight as it may cause further damage. Then immediately call your vet and have him check for damage. He may use an opthalmascope. If there is a foreign object in the eye clean Castor Oil can be used to float it to the surface so that it can be removed without damaging the eye. A herbal wash containing Calendula, Golden Seal and Rescue Remedy is useful for getting rid of minor infections and soothing and healing sore and swollen eyes. The eye is a delicate organ and ulceration can easily occur if injuries, infections or inflammations are left untreated. Veterinary attention and diagnosis is important.

SCOURING

If a horse is scouring and appears systemically ill, that is off feed, appears to be in pain or has a temperature, it would be wise to consult an experienced equine veterinarian as a matter of urgency.

Whilst it is most important to ascertain the underlying causes of scouring - it is also important to treat it symptomatically to start with.

This can be done by feeding Slippery Elm Bark powder combined with PLAIN yoghurt (with acidophilus, bifidus and casei) such as Jalna brand - 2 tablespoons of powder with 2 tablespoons of yoghurt and 1 tablespoon of melted raw honey given in the feed. If they won't eat it - add a little water and give as a drench.

Causes of scouring vary and include ulcerated gut, imbalanced bacteria levels, poisoning, after affects of paraffin drench and tapeworm. Prescribed internal herbal treatment may be necessary to complete healing.

BITES, STINGS, ALLERGIES AND ITCHINESS

It is very easy to grow Aloe Vera cactus plants around the stables and the gel inside is perfect for applying to any of the above to soothe and heal. Hypericum Oil is also useful as an external first aid measure for symptomatic relief. If a horse is hot and agitated from an allergic reaction give 60ml Chamomile Tea internally using a syringe as well as Rescue Remedy. If relief is not obtained after two dosages half an hour apart, seek veterinary attention as a single cortisone injection is often sufficient to settle a once off allergic reaction. However long or medium term use is contra-indicated.

HOOF PROBLEMS

First aid treatment of abscesses, seedy toe, bruised soles, corns, thrush and nail prick/bind is outlined in the chapter - No Foot No Horse.

RESCUE REMEDY

See full details in the chapter The Bach Flower Essences.

WHAT YOU NEED IN YOUR FIRST AID KIT

ITEMS TO PURCHASE AT CHEMIST AND SUPERMARKET

Castor Oil, Eucalyptus Oil, Hydrogen Peroxide, Epsom Salts, Washing Soda, roll of cotton wool, roll of gauze covered cotton padding (Gamgee), waxed non stick squares (to put on wounds under bandages), rolls of sticking plaster, sets of 4 polo or similar bandages (preferably polo), 2 sets of fybagee or similar pads to go under bandages, cold packs, sharp scissors, assortment of syringes 100ml to 2.5ml, plastic medicine cups.

ITEMS TO PURCHASE FROM OTHER SUPPLIERS

Stethoscope, Thermometer, Raw Honey.

OINTMENTS

Arnica, Comfrey, Calendula, Witch Hazel, Thuja.

OILS

Citronella, Pennyroyal, Comfrey, Hypericum

DRIED HERBS

Flowers of Chamomile, Rosehips granules, Wormwood leaf, Slippery Elm Bark Powder, Garlic granules.

HERBAL EXTRACTS

Devil's Claw, Calendula and Yarrow, Calendula and Golden Seal, Calendula

HOMEOPATHICS

Arnica 6C in liquid form

BACH FLOWER ESSENCES

Rescue Remedy, Crab Apple

7 THE BACH FLOWER ESSENCES

The Bach flower essences are an essential part of today's holistic approach to healing horses.

Developed by the highly successful bacteriologist and homeopathic physician Dr Edward Bach in the UK in the 1930s, the Bach flower essences are now universally popular. At the age of 43 Bach gave up his lucrative Harley Street practice to spend the last 6 years of his life developing these unique remedies.

"Flower essences are not homeopathic, herbal or aromatic in their preparation. They are similar to homeopathics in that they are vibrational in nature and physically dilute." (4)

Today the Bach Flower remedies are still prepared from wild flowers, using the same locations and the original methods of Dr Edward Bach, by the Bach Centre in Oxfordshire.

They have been found to be extremely effective for horses and other animals who often react more quickly to them than humans do.

HOW DO THE BACH FLOWER ESSENCES WORK?

The Bach flower essences work in the body by balancing the positive and negative energies in the being concerned.

"They do not act by the roundabout route via the physical body, but at more subtle levels directly influencing the energy system ..."(12)

Bach's concepts of diagnosis were not based on physical symptoms but exclusively on the states of disharmony in the soul, or negative feelings. The simple natural methods used to release the healing energies of the flowers results in them acting directly harmonising and healing.

They are perfectly safe to use - if the remedy is not appropriate, it will do nothing. The appropriate remedies may give extremely rapid results or may take up to 3 months to work. It is a gentle process, a steady development of the positive side of the being. There can be no overdosage, no side effects and no incompatibility with other methods of treatment.

Bach flowers work especially well when used on both sides of a partnership - for example horse and rider.

There are 38 Bach flower essences, 37 being flowers of wild plants, bushes and trees Bach selected from species which are non-toxic in their natural states. Water coming out through rock - Rockwater - is the last.

RESCUE REMEDY

The most famous of the Bach flower remedies is Rescue Remedy. It is a combination of five of the essences - Cherry Plum, Clematis, Impatiens, Rock Rose and Star of Bethlehem, working together as one. Rescue Remedy is applicable to any situation where shock, panic, trauma and or stress of any kind is involved. The faster it is given the better. "Rescue Remedy has saved the lives of many animals in acute conditions". (12) However combinations of the individual flower essences can be used years later to mitigate the after effects of shock, panic and stress.

The essences are given as a few drops in water and syringed directly into the mouth or they can be rubbed into a pulse straight or added to the food or water. Rescue Remedy is also available in a cream for external use but the drops can be added to compresses, washes or herbal treatments for external use as well.

It is a good idea to have several dosage bottles of Rescue

Remedy on hand so that they can be easily and quickly accessed if needed - for horses and people. Keep one in the tack room, one in the first aid kit, one in the house and one in your handbag. Keep out of sunlight in a cool place and shake before use. Purchase a 30ml bottle of Rescue Remedy, three 100ml brown glass medicine bottles with dropper tops, one bottle of still spring water and a small bottle of brandy or organic apple cider vinegar. Fill the bottles seven-eighths with the spring water, one-eighths with brandy (or organic apple cider vinegar) and add 10 drops of the Rescue Remedy. This is the dosage bottle. Squeeze a dropper full into a clean plastic medicine cup, egg cup or similar, pick it up in a 10ml syringe and use that to dose the horse. Keep the dropper and contents of the bottle clean . Store bottles in a cool place out of sunlight. The dropper contains about 2ml which is plenty for one dosage.

Dose a horse for stress, shock, trauma, panic IMMEDIATELY, give the second dose 15 minutes later and the third dose 30 minutes later. Maintain treatment up to five times daily for 24 hours or for longer periods at 2 to 3 times daily. Rescue Remedy is also ideal for PREVENTING any or all of these - for example before travelling, on arrival at a show or anything (such as surgery) which is likely to produce stress, trauma, panic or shock.

If it is necessary for a horse to receive an injection, always give Rescue Remedy immediately beforehand and again 15 minutes later. Injections produce metabolic shock and routinely given weaken the immune system.

Special mixtures of Bach flower essences for each individual horse can be made up in the same way as for Rescue Remedy using the most appropriate selection from the 38 Bach Flower essences. Try to limit the number of essences in a mixture to five. When including Rescue Remedy in a mixture count it as one essence.

WHICH REMEDIES TO CHOOSE?

There are many different interpretations as to the selection of the various essences applicable to humans. For horses and other animals treatment is made in the same way as for humans, the aim being to select the essences most applicable to their negative behaviour. Holistic veterinarians use the Bach flower essences widely.

The following is a guide to help horse owners make an appropriate selection of Bachs to obtain and use. This guide has been developed according to my own experiences. Other selections may be just as effective for certain individual horses. There are many publications about Bachs for humans and animals now available.

My guide divides the remedies into four groups - FEAR, LOW ENERGY, HORSES BEHAVING BADLY and EXCESS ENERGY.

FEAR

Agrimony, Aspen, Cerato, Cherry Plum, Elm, Heather, Larch, Mimulus, Mustard, Red Chestnut, Rock Rose, Scleranthus and Water Violet.

Agrimony is used in herb form more commonly than as a Bach for horses but its main application is for horses that internalise stress. Aspen is most applicable to horses as it is for fear of the unknown or apprehension. Useful as part of a mixture for nervous horses and for competition days. Good for horses that habitually shy.

Cerato is effective for horses that are easily distracted, either during training or at a competition.

Cherry Plum is excellent for horses that panic and/or tend to lose control in a stressful situation or a situation they regard as being stressful. For example racehorses who play up going into the barriers, horses who are poor travellers, horses whose behaviour changes as soon as they get to a competition. Often used together with Rock Rose.

Elm is for fear of responsibility so is especially indicated for the horse that becomes anxious at competitions or travelling to them.

Heather is for fear of being alone and shows up as excessive whinnying in those horses that have to be with their mate - or else! Needs to be given continuously for 3 months, usually with others for dependence, for example Centaury.

Larch is for lack of confidence and is very good for horses that have been abused in the past and for competition horses who are timid or who just need to be bolder. An excellent remedy for many horses.

Mimulus is for known fears. Often used with Aspen. One of the best and most widely used Bachs for horses for obvious reasons.

Mustard is mainly useful for hormone balancing in mares together with herbs. However consider Mustard along with Gorse for depression caused by chronic illness.

Red Chestnut is for over concern for the welfare of others. Especially for horses overly anxious about their foals, or their owners or their mates and who do not tolerate separation well.

Rock Rose is for extreme fear, terror and panic. Indicated for horses that sweat when they panic and who have a strongly developed flight response. Often used with Cherry Plum. Both of these part of Rescue Remedy.

Scleranthus is for loss of balance and lack of co-ordination so is especially indicated in treatment of physical illness.

Water Violet is for fear of damage from others. This is excellent when horses have been injured physically by other horses or physically or emotionally by people. Also for horses that are aloof and don't want to be part of the herd.

Horses that need treatment with Bach flowers for fear of different kinds are all experiencing depletion of adrenal energy to some extent and Rosehips are also indicated.

LOW ENERGY

Centaury, Chestnut Bud, Clematis, Crab Apple, Gorse, Honeysuckle, Hornbeam, Oak, Olive, Sweet Chestnut, Walnut and Wild Rose

Centaury is for the submissive horse that is at the bottom of the pecking order and needs to learn to defend itself better. For example a young horse that is still making foal faces long after it should have stopped! Also for extreme dependence. Centaury is the opposite of Vine.

Chestnut Bud is for the slow learner so is useful in training and behaviour modification. To help break bad habits use with Star of Bethlehem, Honeysuckle and Rockwater for 3 months continuously.

Clematis is one of the flowers in Rescue Remedy for possible loss of consciousness. On its own it is for lack of energy in the present so is useful to aid trauma recovery, for example from colic, long term drug usage: or to help in training when a horse is indifferent and has his mind elsewhere.

Crab Apple is a cleansing flower which is excellent as part of a cleaning and healing wash for external use on wounds and skin infections. Also used internally as part of detoxification treatment after poisoning or excessive drug use. It is highly eliminatory and also causes emotional cleansing so it can occasionally produce behavioural changes or mood swings. For this reason give with Rescue Remedy.

Gorse is for very great hopelessness. Highly indicated if a horse is not recovering well from illness and does not want to eat. It will encourage effort to want to heal, especially if given with the herbs Parsley, Sage and Yarrow.

Honeysuckle is very good for horses that have had bad experiences in the past and are therefore anxious. Also use for episodes such as going to a new home or owner, to the trainer or to a competition.

Hornbeam is wonderful for horses who are mentally and

physically exhausted, through illness or possibly from boredom and/or inappropriate training. Can work quickly so there is no need to continue usage after the desired effects have been achieved.

Oak is for valiant horses that keep on going physically even if they are despondent. Rebuilds physical strength so is good for horses that require stamina such as racehorses, eventers and endurance horses.

Olive is for mental and physical exhaustion usually caused from chronic illness. Useful to give to horses who are suffering post-viral syndrome.

Sweet Chestnut applies to the emotional state of extreme despair and desolation having reached the limit of endurance. Very good for a horse which is being saved from conditions of abuse or a horse that is depressed from illness or unhappy with its circumstances.

Walnut is a powerful protective remedy and link breaker. So it is indicated for sensitive horses that are influenced easily by circumstances. Very good as part of a mixture for travel, competitions, surgery, changes in circumstances and also for training.

Wild Rose is for very low energy and passive disobedience. Can be very useful for the lazy, apathetic or stubborn horse that is difficult to motivate.

Once energy levels have returned, there is no need to continue giving the Bach flower essences for this purpose.

HORSES BEHAVING BADLY

Chicory, Gentian, Holly, Pine, Willow

Chicory is for extreme possessiveness. A good example for use with horses is for mares who want other mares' foals and may cause damage trying to possess them. But it can apply to possessiveness in other areas as well.

Gentian is for nastiness. The horse uses the defence of

kicking, biting, striking etc. to keep people and or horses away.

Holly is for aggressiveness and anger. Also for suspicion and hatred. This may show up as self damage as well as violence to people or other horses and animals. Give with Rescue Remedy to mitigate the effects of anger being released.

Pine is not so much used for horses. The main indication would be for horses who accept bad treatment from their owners. In humans it is used for feelings of unworthiness, guilt and self reproach.

Willow is for resentment in any form. The attitude is likely to be bitter and can be revengeful as well. For example laying ears back, trying to kick and bite, general warning to stay away.

The behaviour of horses in need of Gentian, Willow and Holly has been created by bad treatment, chronic illness, poor conditions and even incorrect feeding. There is always a reason why horses exhibit angry or aggressive behaviour. Very rarely is there a horse that is naturally bad.

EXCESS ENERGY

Beech, Impatiens, Rockwater, Vervain, Vine, White Chestnut and Wild Oat

Beech is for intolerance - of people, animals, the environment and circumstances. Useful for horses who don't like anyone except their master and in the treatment of allergies.

Impatiens as the name implies is for impatience as well as irritability and nervousness. One of the five ingredients in Rescue Remedy. Widely used for horses who want to rush everything - for example pawing, digging holes. It often extends to the intestines as well showing up as loose manure especially as part of competition anxiety.

Rockwater is for extreme energy of the will and inflexibility. As the name implies it is not made from a plant but from water which can wear away the hardest rock. Always used as part of a mixture for degenerative joint disease and together with Star of Bethlehem, Honeysuckle and Chestnut Bud to help break old habits.

Vervain is for over conscientiousness and excessive nervous energy. Very useful for many horses who are highly strung and use up their excess energy in fence walking for example. Also for those big hearted horses who are prone to overdoing things and straining themselves physically. Always used as part of a mixture for arthritis.

Vine is for horses who are extremely dominant and can therefore be difficult to train. Once they learn to work with you they are often amongst the best horses because of their toughness and good brains. The opposite of Centaury.

White Chestnut is useful for horses that tend to be anxious for no apparent reason and have difficulty in concentrating and focusing during training.

Wild Oat is not much used for horses although it has applications for horses who are unfulfilled - for example the retiree who is bored and obviously does not appreciate these circumstances. Sometimes useful for low libido in stallions.

It was Dr Edward Bach's wish that his remedies would be universally accessible, for people to use in healing and self-healing. "To use the Bach remedies successfully calls for no training in medicine or psychology, but for perceptiveness, the ability to think and appreciate, and above all a natural sensitivity and feeling for the other being." (12)

However it is rather difficult to be objective and subjective at the same time so professional assistance in choosing the appropriate Bach flower remedies for your horses and yourself is a good option to consider.

8 HERBAL ALTERNATIVES TO DRUGS

Whilst the quick action of drugs is often necessary to relieve an acute condition symptomatically and in the short term, the negative side effects and contraindications for their use in the long term are well known and documented. There are many conditions which will benefit from herbal remedies for mid to long term treatment, as soon as the prescribed drugs have done their valuable work. The major benefits of correctly prescribed herbal treatments are that they treat the cause of the problem, stimulate and assist the body in the healing process and there is virtually no risk of complications.

Drugs can cause depletion of minerals, antagonism of vitamins, impaired absorption, decreased transport and utilisation of nutrients and have a negative effect on the storage of many nutrients.

The joys and pitfalls of commonly used drugs - corticosteroid hormones, anti-inflammatories and antibiotics are worth studying, so you can make informed decisions about the treatment of your horses.

Corticosteroid hormones are commonly used to treat itchy skin allergies, inflammation of joints and tendon sheaths and chronic lung conditions.

Known side effects of corticosteroids when used in the medium to long term include suppression of the immune system, weakening of muscles and loss of muscle mass, mood swings, weakening of bones and degeneration of joints and tendons. (9)

The herb Liquorice stimulates the body's own production of cortisone and may often be indicated where a condition which has responded to cortico-steroid medication returns upon cessation of the treatment. However the herbs to be selected are going to be influenced by the body system that is going wrong.

In the case of allergies where it is often difficult to determine the cause and where symptoms may affect several body systems, Liquorice may be a good choice together with specifics. In the case of allergies resulting in skin itchiness - herbs to choose from would include Chamomile, Vervain, Euphorbia, Fenugreek, Garlic and Aloes internally as well as Golden Seal, Calendula and St John's Wort externally. In the case of allergies affecting the respiratory system herbs to choose from would include Euphorbia, Elecampagne, Grindelia, Garlic and Horseradish. Support for the immune system is also essential in the treatment of allergies and lung conditions, using herbs such as Echinacea and Rosehips.

Herbs for the treatment of inflammation anywhere in the musculo-skeletal system include Devil's Claw, Guaiacum, Burdock, Tansy, Celery, Juniper, Horsetail and Comfrey but need to be chosen according to the individual condition. The big point to realise is that these herbs don't just relieve inflammation they stimulate and assist the body to complete the healing process.

The non-steroidal anti-inflammatory drugs, which also provide a high degree of relief from pain are very necessary in the relief of trauma and acute lameness. However abuse of these drugs often leads to masking of serious underlying conditions, such as infection or fractures, which require different or additional treatment.

"Long term use or use in very sensitive horses can cause irritation of the lining of the stomach and intestine and occasionally severe intestinal malfunction. Blood and bone marrow abnormalities may sometimes be associated with phenylbutazone therapy." (6)

Another side effect is internal bleeding in the lungs and associated structures including small and large blood vessels.

If anti-inflammatories are needed in the short or medium term, Devil's Claw is the herb to seriously consider. Professional help also can be sought in the choice of other herbs already mentioned. If it is necessary to give non-steroidal

anti-inflammatories even in the short term, feed
2 tablespoons of plain yoghurt (containing acidophilus, bifidus
and casei) twice daily during the course of the treatment to
reduce the negative affects.

ANTIBIOTICS

It is common knowledge in today's world
that the pathogenic organisms which antibiotics
have been designed to fight, are becoming
increasingly resistant to these drugs. These
bacteria can mutate a lot faster than the scientists
can produce new drugs. It is for this reason that
many people are looking back into the future for
alternatives to the treatment of infection. One of
the most detrimental facts in relation to the use and abuse of
anti-biotics are their momentous over prescribing, especially
for minor conditions and the common return of symptoms
after treatment ceases or further down the track.

Also there are undesirable side effects such as liver and
kidney toxicity, skin rashes and suppression of normal bone
marrow functioning, just to name a few.

There are many wonderful herbs which are particularly
effective in dealing with viral and bacterial infections wherever
they may occur in the body. These herbs include Garlic, Red
Clover, Echinacea, Guaiacum, Nettles, Rue, Horsetail,
Dandelion, Agrimony, Burdock, Tansy, Cornsilk, Clivers, Uva
Ursi and Celery. The herbs must be chosen carefully
depending upon the individual condition and individual
prescribing is necessary.

"Drugs are constantly being developed and others which
were previously only available to doctors are being made
available to veterinarians. Many of them are unsuitable for use
in the horse because of their side effects, and consequently we
often fall back on the basics such as penicillin and

sulphonamides." (6)

There are often problems just administering drugs by injection. Muscle pain at the site of the injection is a common problem which can complicate into infection or abscess.

Herbal medicines are extremely non-invasive to administer - being syringed over the tongue - which in the vast majority of cases does not present a problem. In this way the herbs are easily and quickly absorbed by the body and there is no shock to the metabolism as is the case with an injection. The skin is a protective organ and when it is pierced, it is quite natural for the body to register a reaction.

Horses may react severely to penicillin injections. Once a horse has had an allergic reaction, it must never be given a penicillin injection again. Symptoms include highly elevated heart and respiration rate, sweating, veins standing out, usually accompanied by blind galloping. I have seen a horse rear over backwards, then bolt widely and somersault over a gate in blind terror and panic seconds after a penicillin injection. Fortunately the leadrope got caught in the gate which stopped him long enough for us to catch him and put him in the stable to recover. He was treated with Rescue Remedy at 10 minute intervals until his heart and respiratory rate slowed to normal. He was then hosed down as he was in a muck sweat, hand walked and rugged normally. It was a miracle he did not sustain any major injury, but this is the great danger. If a horse has to have a penicillin injection, or any injection for that matter, administer Rescue Remedy FIRST, ensure he is in a safe confined area and get someone exceptionally strong to hold the horse just in case. I have seen another horse react to penicillin and realising the problem, I was able to instruct the handler to hold on no matter what, which he did and we were able to get the horse calmed down quite quickly. Another common reaction to injections of drugs or earlier vaccines is widespread swelling (oedema). Immediately give Rescue Remedy and call your vet. "There may be oedema of the eyelids and elsewhere, while released fluid in or about the respiratory tract may cause respiratory distress. The sudden appearance of extensive oedema should be regarded with concern and veterinary advice sought immediately." (6)

There is a grave danger of horses being poisoned if they accidentally eat processed feeds containing hormones or antibiotics which are intended for other livestock such as pigs, poultry or cattle. Symptoms may appear immediately or several months after exposure. "Horses present symptoms of posterior weakness, profuse sweating, occasionally muscular tremors and dark brown urine. There can be permanent damage to heart muscle, but toxicity may be arrested in the early stages by removing the stomach contents and feeding mineral oil." (6) Death can occur. There will be liver damage. If poisoning is suspected, administer Rescue Remedy and call your vet immediately. I have heard of horses which were poisoned from eating processed equine feeds which had apparently been contaminated from other stock feeds left in the mixing equipment.

Herbal remedies can be used in association with veterinary treatment to treat poisoning. I was involved with a case of botulism which was resolved successfully with expert veterinary care and attention, brilliant management on the part of the owners and specially prescribed herbal medicine for detoxification and physical and mental support. To add to the difficulties the mare was pregnant but subsequently delivered a healthy foal!

Veterinary treatment and herbal medicine can and does exist successfully side by side. The incidence of this co-operation is increasing all the time, for the greater benefit of our equine friends.

9 HERBAL WORMING

There are a number of herbs which will kill worms in the gut and expel them from the body, known respectively as vermicides and vermifuges. These include Wormwood (surprise surprise), Garlic, Tansy, Rue, Aloes, Fennel, Male Fern and Cayenne. Seeds of pumpkin, parsley, mustard, melon, aniseed and pomegranate and a number of grasses and shooting leaves of hedges and trees also have the same effect. The latter include mustard, couch grass, brambles, broom tops, ash twigs and elder. (3)

Wormwood has been used successfully for threadworms and roundworms; Garlic for roundworms, pinworms, tapeworms and hookworms (4); Tansy, Rue and Aloes for all types of worms and Male Fern for tapeworms (3). There is anecdotal evidence to suggest that Red Clover is effective against redworms, probably due to its high copper content.

Redworms, also known as bloodworms or large strongyles and bots are the most difficult to eradicate using herbs. Therefore it is definitely not advisable to rely completely on herbal worming. However the incidence of chemical worming may be considerably reduced, provided good management is in place.

The best way to give herbs for worming purposes is to make up a dried mixture and feed it as part of the feed over two feeds. Most horses are happy to eat the herbs when given in this way. For fussy eaters it can be fed in smaller amounts over four feeds mixed in with only part of the feed with strong molasses water and the rest of the feed given later.

On properties where there are larger numbers of horses which are not on hard feed, the dried herbs can be made into a tea and drenched using a stomach tube, provided there is a competent person to do this.

RECIPE FOR HERBAL WORMING MIX

Fennel Seeds (40g/1½oz), Tansy Seeds or Flowers or Mixture of both (35g/1¼oz), Rue (40g/1½oz), Wormwood (25g/¾oz), Red Clover (30g/1oz), Garlic (30g/1oz). This mixture weighs 200g (7oz) and is sufficient for a horse weighing from 350kg to 650kg (770-1430lb) (14.2 hands and upwards). For horses and ponies weighing 300kg (660lb) or less (14.2 hands and under), use half this amount per dosage. For Shetlands and Miniatures use a quarter of this amount per dosage. At the same time give 20g (¾oz) Aloes powder stirred thoroughly into a small tin of pureed apple baby food, administered in a 60ml syringe. Give the full dose for the full sized horse, half for the medium sized horse and quarter for the little ones. You can also follow up with another dosage of Aloes 10 days after the original worming for extra efficacy. Aloes is extremely bitter and this is the only way to get it into the horse successfully!

PREGNANT MARES - CAUTIONS

Wormwood, Aloes and Rue should NOT be administered to pregnant mares as they are muscle stimulants. The uterus is quite muscular and they could cause contractions. Garlic can be fed to pregnant mares up to a month before foaling and re-commenced a month after foaling. This is to prevent the garlic coming through in the milk when the foal is very young.

MANAGEMENT

Bot eggs should be removed daily with a bot knife. The flies can be deterred from laying eggs by using a herbal insect repellent especially drenching the legs. Recipe - 500ml (17½fl oz) spray pack - half water (or strained Wormwood tea) half organic apple cider vinegar, add 15 drops Oil of Citronella, 5 drops Pennyroyal Oil.

The horse's anus and surrounds should be regularly washed (especially if there are signs of rubbing) as the pinworm lays its eggs here which causes itching.

Where horses are kept in yards and small paddocks, especially if there is more than one horse, all manure should be picked up and removed daily. Paddocks where horses are kept should be harrowed and routinely spelled or cattle should be grazed at the same time or run through after the horses have been moved.

Garlic should be fed routinely (1 tablespoon fresh crushed or dried granulated daily for a 450kg [990lb] horse) as part of a management program in conjunction with herbal worming.

HOW OFTEN TO WORM?

This depends entirely on the level of management, seasonal conditions and stocking rates. On coastal country where there is a heavy population of horses with poor management and hot, wet conditions, obviously the incidence of worming will need to be much more frequent than a property where there are only a few horses with very good management and a mild, dry climate. Where it is known that worm populations are high, worming would need to be carried out every 4 weeks with a 10 day follow up to pick up larvae which have hatched in the meantime. In ideal conditions every 12 weeks will be adequate.

Regular fecal testing is highly recommended as a management tool to determine incidence of worming necessary.

Other advantages of using herbal worming mixtures are that they give the horses' gut a good spring cleaning and also help move sand through especially if boiled linseeds or cold pressed linseed oil are also fed routinely.

Herbal worming mixtures are pasture friendly and do not remove dung beetles from the soil. However you may end up with a few Fennel and Tansy plants!

With worms building up resistance to conventional anthelmintics, herbal worming is a viable part of control with additional benefits, but some important cautions.

The best time to worm is close to the full moon, say the day before and the day of the full moon. French folklore has it that this is the time the worms are on the move and this is also put to good use by organic gardeners. The cycle of the moon is every 28 days. It is not essential to worm at this time.

10 HOW TO PREVENT and TREAT COMMON PROBLEMS

Without sport the modern horse would not exist. But the demands made by man on horses in sport today are creating new problems - in just the same way that competition, stress and modern living affects us. Horses in sport are subjected to a rat race made for them by man! A small percentage succeed and become winners, but the attrition rate is high.

In the racing industry wastage is high across the world. In Australia figures compiled by the VRC in 1983 showed that only 60% of mares served produced live foals, 17% of foals died before 12 months, wastage continued as yearlings and later so that only 30% of foals actually raced. (7)

Just like the human athlete the equine athlete often succumbs to health problems at vital moments in their careers - before a big race, on the way to an important competition for example - just when peak performance is expected and has been carefully planned for.

"When a horse fails to live up to its apparent potential the problem is rarely a lack of fitness. Instead, the cause usually lies in limitations that fall into the categories of disease and pathology. Subtle defects in the bones of the leg or in the airways of the respiratory system appear to be surprisingly common sources of limitation in top horses." (2)

The best way to ensure optimum performance is to avoid problems occurring in the first place. From a naturopathic point of view this means looking after the whole horse, all the time ...

The three points of the triangle (see over) affect the overall health of the horse at all times and often affect more than one body system at a time. Balancing the various body systems is essential to vitality. A horse can be in a chronic state of ill health, have no named disease, the usual tests may only show

THE HEALTH TRIANGLE

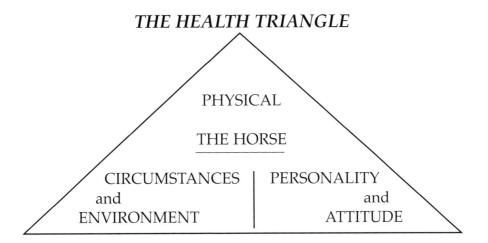

vague abnormalities if any, or he may be in a state of rude, bounding good health. The shades of grey between the black and white are many. Understanding these shades of grey and learning how to keep them tipped to the positive is one of the secrets of producing that super equine athlete many people are striving for. Feeding more and more high powered feeds and injecting horses with uppers and downers is not the answer.

In the following chapters I will look at the body systems of the horse and explain how to read warnings that the horse may be heading in the wrong direction. The earlier problems and imbalances are treated the more likely they can be fully resolved without rearing their ugly head at a later date, usually at a moment of maximum inconvenience.

I will also make some suggestions for treating common problems and explain when it is wiser to call for professional help. When I am asked to treat a horse for a client I always take into account the three points of the health triangle and treat the whole horse at the one time for every aspect of his health which needs attention. I always use a combination of herbal extracts, Bach flower essences and a completely natural feeding and supplements program. The body systems are in a constant state of interaction which is why this kind of holistic treatment is so important.

It is lucky for the horse that he can earn his living in today's world. Despite the negative aspects many horses lead much easier lives than they would have in the wild, although it is debatable whether they are happier or even healthier. The modern horse is fed and sheltered but still allowed to indulge in some of their natural instincts. It is keeping this balance between nature and the demands made by man of today's sport horse that is essential if he wants a winner - a horse that is healthy in mind and body.

11 NO FOOT - NO HORSE

One of the oldest and truest adages of all time - there are myriad problems which afflict the foot of the horse - abscesses, bruised soles, corns, seedy toe, wall separation, thrush, cracks, poor hoof quality, slow growth and so on. It is a good idea to become familiar with the symptoms and causes of these problems, so that they can be prevented or remedied before conditions worsen. No foot - no horse.

ABSCESSES

These can develop from punctures of the sole, subsolar bruising, corns and close nails. Some horses are prone to them without obvious cause. Acute and extreme lameness shows up suddenly with an abscess. An indication of inflammation of the hoof capsule is the distention and pulsation of the artery running down the inside of the horse's leg (best felt just above the fetlock joint). Your vet or farrier will usually be able to find the abscess using hoof testers and release the infection by making a discreet drainage hole. DO NOT ALLOW ANYTHING BUT A TINY PARING OF THE AREA TO MAKE THE DRAINAGE HOLE OR THE SENSITIVE TISSUE CAN BE DAMAGED CAUSING FURTHER LONG LASTING PROBLEMS. Usually it is best if the shoe is removed so the foot can be hot tubbed twice daily using Epsom salts (big handful to 6 litres [UK 10½pt; US 13pt] of water). The drainage hole should be syringed out with Hydrogen Peroxide and then poulticed using plugs of cotton wool soaked in Castor Oil and the whole foot bandaged to prevent dirt from entering. If no drainage hole has been made the foot should still be hot tubbed. Quick action should prevent the abscess breaking out on the coronet band and treatment should continue until the horse is sound (up to 10 days). Feed a heaped tablespoon dried granulated or freshly crushed garlic twice daily for a 450kg (990lb) horse for 2 weeks. Expert farrier care is essential.

Horses prone to recurring abscesses should be treated with a prescribed blood cleansing herbal mixture for 12 weeks for resolution of infection, provision of copper and prevention of abscesses recurring in the future.

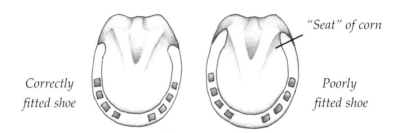

Correctly fitted shoe

"Seat" of corn

Poorly fitted shoe

BRUISED SOLES/CORNS

Flat footed, thin soled horses are more prone to bruising than others. Causes of bruising are stones, excessive work on hard ground or poorly fitting shoes which cause a repetitive trauma. A corn is a bruise which occurs between the wall and bar of the foot at the so-called seat of a corn. Lameness is usually worse on hard ground and is much less obvious on soft ground. It may also be intermittent or worse on turns or show up as a restricted stride especially on turns plus a lack of willingness to extend the stride. Treatment for corns is the same as for abscess if the corn has become infected, together with expert farrier care . The bruising should be treated to resolve it quickly by dosing with 1ml homeopathic Arnica 6C internally hourly for 3 hours as soon as the problem occurs, followed by dosage 2 to 3 times daily for at least one week. Corns which have not become infected can have Arnica ointment applied to them topically as well.

SEEDY TOE/WALL SEPARATION

When the wall separates at the toe, the condition is called seedy toe. Anaerobic bacteria thrive in this area causing the condition to spread. Expert farrier care is essential to cut out the dead hoof. The holes should be syringed with straight hydrogen peroxide once daily, filled with straight copper sulphate and plugged with medicated peat moss or cotton wool and anhydrous wool fat. A mixture of raw honey and copper sulphate is also worthwhile.

When the wall separates at the quarters it is most commonly called White Line Disease and a cheesy type substance is present in the hoof wall. Treatment is the same as for seedy toe. This condition, if left untreated, can have dire consequences. Large areas of the foot can be eaten away with the huge risk of infection. Expert farrier care is needed. Special shoes and applications of artificial hoof material may also be required. Internal herbal treatment is the same as for abscesses. To encourage faster and better quality hoof growth Rosehips and Comfrey should be added to the diet and Comfrey Oil used externally on the coronet band, frog and bulbs of the feet. Comfrey should only be added to the diet once all risk of infection has been ruled out.

THRUSH

This condition which is characterised by an accumulation of black, foul-smelling moist material in the clefts of the frog is prevented by keeping hooves well picked out and by not allowing horses to stand in dirty, moist conditions. Treatment requires a clean dry bed, twice daily picking and brushing out of the hooves and applying straight Eucalyptus Oil once daily. It is antiseptic and anti-fungal. If thrush is allowed to progress it can extend into the sensitive tissues and cause lameness and further infection. Do not apply straight Eucalyptus Oil to the skin as it will burn and cause great discomfort. See greasy heel and mud fever.

CRACKS

These occur vertically in the hoof wall and extend upwards (grasscrack) or develop at the coronary band and extend downwards (sandcrack). The latter develop as a result of injury to the coronary band. Grasscracks are usually the result of the foot being overgrown and splitting. Severe cracks may extend into the sensitive tissue causing lameness and exposing the horse to risk of infection. Expert farrier care is essential, especially to immobilise cracks if possible. If there is no infection present daily application of raw linseed oil or mixed with an equal amount of Comfrey oil will make the foot more flexible and accelerate growth rate. Feed Rosehips granules at the rate of 2 tablespoons twice daily (for an average sized horse 450kg/990lb) for at least 12 weeks to improve the quality of the horn.

BRITTLE FEET, SLOW GROWTH, POOR HORN QUALITY

Same treatment as for Cracks and expert farrier care.

NAIL PRICK/BIND

The horse will exhibit varying degrees of lameness and will quite often be severely lame and in great pain - the nail must be removed and the hole flushed out with Venice Turpentine which has been heated up to make it runny. Or the shoe may need to be removed and same treatment given as for abscesses.

With any of the preceding conditions ensure that horses receive their Tetanus shots if they are not current.

HOOF DRESSING

To keep horses' feet from drying out apply olive oil or raw linseed oil or a mixture of both daily to the coronet band, frog and bulbs after picking out. Do not apply to the sole as this is the area where the horse takes in and gives out moisture. "Never use petroleum based products on horses' hooves."(10)

In dry weather let troughs overflow so that the horses can stand in some mud for a while each day to help rehydrate hooves. Choice of bedding is important for horses that are continuously stabled. "Sawdust, shavings and rice hulls all pull water out of the hoof and can cause considerable problems with dryness. Straw does not pull water out of the hoof and is therefore a better choice in these circumstances."(10)

In wet weather ensure hooves are cleaned out and dried well before stabling at night. Paddock horses need a dry area to shelter in these conditions.

COPPER DEFICIENCY

Horses prone to thrush, seedy toe and abscesses are usually lacking adequate copper in their diet. This can be rectified by feeding Rosehips granules at the rate of 2 tablespoons twice daily for an average sized horse (450kg/990lb) as well as Australian seaweed.

Calcium and silica are also important minerals for the health of the foot. High grade dolomite fed at the rate of 1 tablespoon twice daily for the average sized horse (450kg/990lb) provides calcium and a little silica. Oats and millet are very high in silica. See feeding sections.

CORRECT SHOEING

It is beyond the scope of this book to fully discuss this important topic. There are many reliable references available. However here are a couple of golden rules to learn, observe in your horses and ensure your farrier applies. "The longer the toe grows the greater the leverage it exerts and the greater the strain put on the tendons. Strain on the tendons is also increased by lowering the heels of the foot to excess. The ideal angle for the front of the hoof varies from one horse to another, depending on the individual's conformation. The angle of the hoof, however, should be the same as that of the pastern (and this in turn is the same as the angle described by the shoulder). Thus a line drawn from the front of the fetlock to the coronary band and then on down the front of the hoof should be straight, with no deflection forwards or backwards at the coronary band." (6)

LAMINITIS

Laminitis, also known as founder, is a potentially life threatening situation. Laminitis is inflammation of the sensitive laminae of the foot and is an extremely painful condition. There is heat in the feet and the pulse in the digital arteries is easy to feel, as discussed under abscesses above. Ponies, especially small ponies and overweight ponies, are particularly susceptible.

The great risk with this condition is that the pedal bone can rotate or sink and penetrate the sole of the foot, which may necessitate putting the horse or pony down.

Major causes are spring and unseasonal flushes in the pasture, over consumption of grain, stress, toxicity, excessive work on hard ground, excessive weightbearing on one leg and retained foetal membranes after foaling.

The first thing to do is to remove the patient from pasture if that is the cause and call your vet. As a first aid measure and to assist treatment generally administer Rescue Remedy and drench liberally with Rosehips tea at regular intervals. This is one of those times when the quick action of non-steroidal anti-inflammatory drugs (veterinary prescribed) is really necessary. The most important thing is to alleviate pain and inflammation rapidly. Once this has been achieved seek professional advice for herbal treatment to continue this as well as improve circulation, provide detoxification and reduce stress. Rosehips is a wonderful herb for Laminitis as it is very high in Vitamin C which is specific for any time of stress and for the exchange between the arterial and venous circulation. This occurs in the dense capillary beds in the foot, the functioning of which is compromised with laminitis. Other herbs which I select from are the circulatory herbs Nettles, Rue, Hawthorn, the liver herbs and the marvellous anti-inflammatory, analgesic and healing herb Devil's Claw.

Expert farrier care and correct management is essential. "The latter entails yarding the horse on deep sand (at least 10 cms) which is kept wet and cool. It is essential that the sand is wet and cool which means the sand and the horse must be under shelter to protect them from the sun especially in the summer. Do not place the horse in hot sand, as this would greatly aggravate the condition. Standing the horse in the wet, cool sand supports the whole foot and helps to take out the inflammation. To help reactivate normal circulation alternately hot and cold tub the feet 10 minutes each alternately three times in succession twice daily. A handful of washing soda could also be added to the water." (10)

Management includes placing in a confined area, perhaps with light hand exercise depending on the case. If very fat limit feed intake to very plain meadow hay or if this difficult to get, good quality straw or wheaten chaff will do especially for ponies.

Once a horse or pony has had an attack of laminitis it is unfortunately a prime candidate for future attacks, so great care must be taken to avoid this happening again. Fortunately there are many happy case outcomes for this serious affliction.

12 THE NERVOUS HORSE

"Horses have been enveloped in human dreams, myths, ambitions, and sentiment for so long that the story we think of as theirs is often but a distorted reflection of our own desires, and then not always our most noble desires." (2)

No matter whether you ride horses just for the love of them or whether you are trying to win an Olympic Gold Medal, our horses are always to a certain extent a reflection of ourselves. With their highly developed flight instinct, they are particularly sensitive to their environment, including the human beings they come into contact with.

As riders and handlers of horses we influence their behaviour more than we realise. This is especially true in relation to their nervous system. The first thing we need to understand is that horses do not think, see, smell, hear or perceive things the way we do. To understand the genetic hardwired behaviour of horses, I highly recommend Stephen Budiansky's book "The Nature of Horses". Once we have grasped the facts in relation to equine behaviour, especially their nervous reactions, we are well on the way to building a harmonious partnership with our horses.

However, horses, like people, will show nervous discontent in particular body areas. There are four main types - those who react in the gut, the skin, the heart or the lungs. They can also be more than one type.

In horses those who show nervous reactions in the gut do so typically by way of loose manure, an excessive number of droppings and sometimes excessive numbers of urinations. These horses can also internalise stress into the gut which if not corrected often manifests as gut ulceration and scouring.

The skin reactors are prone to itchiness, scratching and skin problems. Horses who react in the heart usually adrenalise easily, often taking a long time for the elevated heart rate to

return to normal. Those who react in the lungs tend to be horses who do not breathe deeply and regularly while being ridden. The heart and lung reactors in particular present training and fitness difficulties.

If a horse's nervous system is not balanced, this impairs performance in the sport horse and inhibits enjoyment of the pleasure horse. Obviously the causes of the imbalance need to be discovered and rectified as part of any treatment.

Causes of nervous system imbalances range from inherited behaviour to intolerance of feeds, training methods, riders, handlers, occupation, environment and imbalances in other body systems.

It is surprising how many owners will say "Oh her mother did that as well". I was treating a show hack recently who had a fixation with foals and small horses. She had no apparent hormonal problems and I told the owner I thought it would be pretty difficult to change her obsessive behaviour. As it turned out the combination of herbs and Bach flower essences I chose for her did work and quite quickly. It was only afterwards that the owner discovered and reported to me that the dam of this mare had been the same!

Differentiating soundness and behavioural problems is usually one of the first steps in deciding how to treat apparent nervousness. The main reason humans are able (or in some cases unable) to train horses is the phenomenal memory of the equine species. All the good horsemen know how to use this fact to their advantage. So depending upon each horse's individual degree of sensitivity (temperament), they are a product of what has happened to them in their handling (or mishandling) by man. So whilst actual pain in varying degrees is often the cause of behavioural problems, often it is only the memory of pain associated with bad handling and rough "training" that produces an ongoing nervousness. One stark example of bad handling which stays with horses for life to some degree or other is the practice of giving a shock from a battery (usually to get them out of the barriers).

Treating the memory of pain is where the Bach flower essences in particular often produce astoundingly good results. They are also used for symptomatic treatment in conjunction with nervine herbs which ameliorate symptoms and treat the underlying causes at the same time. Girthiness is a very good example of a problem which can in a mild form be from the memory of pain but is usually from a physical cause. These include unsoundness in the wither, spine and ribs or discomfort coming from the liver and sometimes also the spleen.

Overstimulation of nerve fibres can produce acid wastes in the body and many nervous horses who appear cranky as well as being generally sore are a victim of this problem, usually worsened by inappropriate feeding.

It will be seen from the foregoing that treating a horse for nervousness is not simply a matter of feeding them a few nervine herbs. As with any condition, the whole horse must be evaluated and treated at the same time, to have any chance of successful re-balancing, with the horse ultimately being maintained on a natural diet.

Obviously though, a selection from the nervine herbs will always be part of a mixture for nervous system balancing. There are seven nervine herbs which I use for horses. They are Chamomile, Vervain, Valerian, Mugwort, Skullcap, Hops and Passiflora. I only ever use the nervine herb St Johns Wort externally as part of a treatment for skin conditions.

CHAMOMILE

This herb is specific for the gut reactors and the skin reactors. Any horse which shows loose manure to any degree when nervous is a candidate for Chamomile. Also any horse which reacts easily on the skin to insect bites, flies, ticks or simply from pressure is also in need of Chamomile. This herb is readily available and can very safely be added to the feed by horse owners. One handful flowers of Chamomile twice daily for the average sized horse can be added to the feed straight or made into a tea to extract the medicinal qualities more fully and the whole lot added.

VERVAIN

This herb is for the skin reactor which shows up as itchiness, sensitivity to biting insects, rashes, lumps, sores etc. Also typically the horse in need of Vervain often sweats excessively when nervous and may also tremble or even shake. They may also be impatient, fiddly, fussy and their veins may stand out when they are nervous. Very often these horses are over-conscientious, but use up too much nervous energy before they really need to, say before a race or a competition, so that they haven't got enough fuel left in the tank when it is needed. Vervain is often part of the answer to this kind of nervous temperament.

VALERIAN

This herb is also for the gut reactors. But for those horses that react in the opposite way to the Chamomile horse, by holding their muscles tightly which in turn has a tightening affect on the internal organs including the intestines. These horse are literally "uptight" and typically have manure which is much too hard, tight muscles and a tucked up gut. They may also be prone to tying-up. They may have difficulties in passing manure because of this and may be prone to impaction colic. Valerian has the affect of allowing the horse to relax his whole body after work but to use himself correctly when asked to work, so that ultimately he lets down in the gut. It is contra-indicated for horses that are prone to loose manure or scouring. Valerian is widely used as a sedative for competition horses and is on the swabbing list. It is contra-indicated for horses which have loose manure as a result of nervousness as it will make them worse. Competitors should not regard Valerian as a quick fix for a nervous problem.

PASSIFLORA

This is a very good herb to use as part of a mixture for horses who are generally anxious, apprehensive and never seem to be at ease. I use it a lot for mares, including those who are also being treated for hormonal problems.

MUGWORT

Mugwort is specific for horses who are extremely sensitive and are usually over reactive to some or all of the following stimuli - sight, sound, touch, smell, light, wind and even barometric pressure. Chestnuts, especially Thoroughbreds, while I love them dearly, seem to be prime candidates to benefit from Mugwort!

HOPS

Hops is excellent as part of a mixture when help is needed

to reshape nervous attitudes and old habits. It is excellent for those horses whose heart rates rise noticeably when they are stressed, but who recover quite quickly from these episodes. An old fashioned remedy to calm an excited horse was to give them some beer and Hops are an important ingredient in beermaking!

SKULLCAP

Professional advice should be sought for the use of this herb, as its indications are extremely specific and dosage rates are critical. I use it only as part of a mixture for horses who consistently and seriously over-adrenalise and who do not recover quickly from this nervous state. Their heart rates go up and stay up until the adrenaline works its way out.

All herbs including the nervine herbs have many other beneficial properties.

Nervine herbs work best when given in a mixture with a selection of appropriate Bach flower essences as well as a selection of other herbs to treat the whole horse. All aspects of the horse's metabolism must be brought into balance for a treatment for nervous system problems to be permanently effective. Treatment should be continuous over a full blood cycle (12 weeks) to achieve the best results.

THE NERVOUS RIDER

The influence of the rider on the nervous behaviour of a horse should always be considered as part of the equation. Most thinking riders are aware of the sensitivity of the horse in this regard. For nervous riders, a mixture of Bach flower essences can be

chosen to help them relax and perform better. These benefits flow through to the horse and improves the quality and harmony of the partnership of horse and rider.

There are times when a change of trainer, rider or occupation is the only answer to chronic nervousness. The same horse that was a nervous wreck or a demon with one rider or trainer can be a happy chappy with a different trainer or rider.

Two stories of racehorses illustrate this point overwhelmingly. One was a horse with a history of chronic gut ulceration. He was completely healed until he went back to the trainer who had him when his problems started. Another is a story of a racehorse who was being trained by his owners. They were with the horse in the stables on a raceday when the horse heard his previous trainer speaking loudly at the far end of the line. The horse immediately broke out in a sweat and started shaking.

CONDITIONS OF THE NERVOUS SYSTEM

STRINGHALT

In Australia, Stringhalt is apparently caused from horses ingesting toxins associated with grazing of certain pasture weeds, namely Capeweed and Catsear also known as Flatweed or false Dandelion (Hypocheris radicans). The toxins affect the long nerves in the body. This results in an exaggerated flexion of one or both hind legs, which can be so severe that the front of the fetlock can hit the belly, or the signs may be quite mild. Mild cases are often more noticeable if the horse is asked to back up, or if there is a change of terrain, the weather is cold or if the horse becomes nervously excited for any reason. Although the symptoms of Stringhalt and Locking Patella are not the same, there can be confusion, so it is best to have the condition diagnosed by an expert equine veterinarian, as treatment is quite different. Traditional Stringhalt produces symptoms similar to Australian Stringhalt but usually much less severe; the cause is unknown.

Stringhalt can also result in partial paralysis of the voice box so that the horse becomes a "roarer". Horses with Stringhalt can walk, canter and gallop quite well but they cannot trot properly. Seasonal conditions and copper and magnesium deficiencies in the soil also appear to play a role in its occurrence. If Stringhalt is suspected the first thing to do is immediately remove the horse from the pasture, administer Rescue Remedy, feed a plain diet of good quality meadow hay and add high grade dolomite to drinking water at the rate of one handful to 10 litres (UK 17½pt; US 22pt). Do not confine the horse but allow it to move about as it wishes.

I have treated many horses for stringhalt, the majority of them successfully. In my experience the quicker treatment starts, the better the results. I use a combination of nervine and detoxification herbs as well as Bach flower essences. Two of the most useful nervine herbs in helping to resolve Stringhalt are Valerian for symptomatic relief and Mugwort to help repair the nerve signals. The horses that have not responded to treatment have either been chronic cases afflicted for long periods of time or horses which have apparently not been grazing on either capeweed or catsear. Horses left untreated in any way will become afflicted with muscle wastage. It is important to understand the difference between catsear or false dandelion (Hypochaeris radicans) and the true dandelion (Taraxacum Officinale) - see List of Useful Herbs.

Obviously the best option for prevention of Stringhalt is pasture management to balance the minerals in the soil and prevent the growth of these plants.

If a serious condition of the nervous system is suspected, such as Wobbler's Syndrome, consult an expert equine veterinarian for a diagnosis.

13 THE DIGESTIVE SYSTEM

The digestive system of the horse has its own peculiarities developed from centuries of genetic evolution. Understanding these will help to prevent common problems from occurring especially due to inappropriate feeding and management. Prevention is always better than cure.

"The horse has a completely herbivorous (vegetable) diet and its digestive system has evolved to deal with this type of food material. For example, the large intestine contains a population of microbes which break down the vegetable cellulose." (6)

"And unlike many large grazing animals, horses break down the otherwise indigestible cellulose of stems and leaves in a digestive organ known as the caecum." (1)

"Careful study of the bacterial, physical and biochemical properties of ruminant (sheep, cattle, goats, deer, camels and hippos) and caecal (horses, rhinos and tapirs) digestion has found that their basic mechanism of action is indistinguishable." (2)

"But animal behaviour studies have consistently shown one extremely curious fact : wild equids in competition with ruminants invariably choose the very worst, lowest-protein, highest-fibre roughage." (2)

The horse has evolved over millions of years from a browsing forest animal to an animal grazing over the steppes, savannahs and prairies - upon different kinds of grasses such as wheat, rye, fescue and barley. There is no genetic pressure on them of any kind now that they are provided with grazing and/or hand fed, so those ancient genetically engineered instincts survive to this day.

THE IMPORTANCE OF FEEDING ROUGHAGE

Obviously the modern competition horse needs more energy than the rough grasses the wild horses needed for survival, but the most important point to grasp is that today many horses do not receive sufficient roughage and/or receive too much concentrated and unnatural feeds.

This often leads to problems such as laminitis (especially in ponies), colic, scouring, poor feed conversion, gut ulceration, impaired performance and "behavioural" problems.

There seems to be a general misconception that feeding generous amounts of hay and chaff is a bad thing. As a large percentage of horses today spend most of their time locked up either in stables, yards or small paddocks with virtually no access to grazing, it stands to reason that their natural instinct to spend a large part of their time grazing should be catered for by the provision of roughage in the form of ad lib or several feeds of hay.

A variety of hays can be considered, depending upon the size, condition and work load of the horse concerned. Meadow or grass hay (high in roughage, low in nutrients) is very suitable for all horses regardless and especially ponies tending to be overweight. Oaten hay is useful to feed in conjunction with lucerne chaff and lucerne hay with oaten chaff. Clover hay or a mix of clover and grass hay is also a good hay to feed sparingly but watch out for a high percentage of clover especially red clover in it, as this can be quite heating to some horses (especially ponies) and to some mares due to its high oestrogen content. The amount of protein in high quality lucerne hay can be extremely high (up to 23%), so this factor must be taken into consideration when hay is purchased and any necessary adjustments made to other protein in the diet.

The number of horses who have access on a daily basis to pasture or grassy paddocks are in the minority and they are the lucky ones.

"Przewalski's horses in natural settings will spend half or more of their time in a 24 hour period grazing, and nearly 10% of their time walking or running.
A horse denied the chance to engage in these activities (as are many stabled horses fed concentrated feeds and turned out for only an hour or less a day) may in effect fall into a vicious circle." (2)

THE FIRST STEP OF THE DIGESTIVE PROCESS

Eating grass with its cellulose walls requires a tremendous amount of chewing and the ability to cope with grit which comes along with the grass. The horse's teeth are specially adapted for this - the first step of digestion.

Horses permanently kept in stables and fed uniformly ground cubes and pellets have been observed by horse dentists to have mouths which look as if they are nearly double their real age. Horses such as these are being deprived of the chewing and production of saliva which is the instigation of the digestion process and important to the health of the gastro-intestinal tract.

FACTORS LEADING TO PROBLEMS

Lack of adequate roughage is not the only predisposing factor to problems of the digestive system. Others are ...
* Imbalanced gut flora.
* Lack of adequate exercise.

  * High worm burdens or over-use of chemical wormers.
  * Overfeeding of concentrated feeds and supplements with excess protein, added salt, sugar, preservatives, stabilisers and synthetically produced vitamins and minerals.
  * Repeated shocks to the metabolism by excessive administration of antibiotics, hormones and anti-inflammatories especially by injection.
  * The stress caused to many horses who are locked up for most of their lives manifested externally by weaving, crib biting or wind sucking or internally - leading to laminitis, gut ulceration, colic or scouring.
  * Poisoning.
  * Teeth problems. All horses must have their teeth checked and treated by a reputable horse dentist at six monthly intervals from the age of 2 years onwards.

CONDITIONS OF THE DIGESTIVE SYSTEM

COLIC
Colic is a potentially life threatening condition. In addition to the factors outlined above, there are a few golden rules to avoid colic. Never change diets suddenly - gradually phase in new feeds over a period of 10 days or so starting with small amounts and gradually building up. Always check new feeds for quality (dampness, mould, contamination etc) before feeding out. If in doubt chuck it out! Horses coming in off grass onto hard feeds should have plenty of roughage and bulk in their ration and hard feeds should be introduced a little at a time. Horses coming off hard feeding and being turned out onto good pasture (especially lush ones) should be introduced to grass initially for short periods, gradually increasing the length of the periods, to avoid the possibility of grass staggers or

laminitis as well as colic. Never feed pollard at all - at best it increases acidity and at worst it can cause impaction in the gut. Horses prone to colic should have careful natural feeding programs designed for them individually. Flowers of Chamomile should be fed routinely as a digestive aid at the rate of a handful twice daily either straight or made into a tea for an average sized horse. For horses grazing or living on sandy country cold pressed linseed oil or boiled linseeds should be fed routinely to help move sand through the gut. For the average sized horse 40ml daily of the oil or half a cup dry weight of whole linseeds is sufficient. A current practice of feeding psyllium husks, which are mostly composed of cellulose, for this purpose seems to work well.

SCOURING

The manure of the horse is a very important barometer of its intestinal health. Manure should not be too hard or too loose, too dry or too wet, should not have an offensive odour or a particularly pale or dark unnatural colour. The size of the dropping and the number of droppings per 24 hours are also part of the equation.

If left untreated scouring can become so chronic that the horse cannot remain in work. It is often a sign of a compromised gastro-intestinal tract if not full blown gut ulceration with attendant poor absorption of nutrients and poor feed conversion.

The first thing to do is to administer Rescue Remedy at regular intervals.

It is wise to feed probiotics to try to redress imbalanced bacterial levels in the gut. If this is the case, this treatment should produce an improvement usually within a short space of time and if it is not the case, no harm can be done. Feed 2 tablespoons natural yoghurt (with acidophilus, bifidus and casei) mixed with 1 tablespoon melted raw honey two to three times daily depending on the severity of the condition. This mixture can be syringed into the mouth if the horse will not eat it in his feed.

Feed only meadow hay or grass hay ad lib. Give a small medicinal feed three times daily of good quality oaten or wheaten chaff to which has been added, boiled barley, a little corn (maize) oil, 1 tablespoon high grade dolomite, 1 tablespoon Slippery Elm Bark Powder and 1 tablespoon bentonite . Bran and lucerne must be avoided. For provision of greens - native grasses are ideal but may be difficult to find - kikuyu must be avoided. Try to feed a couple of medium sized Comfrey leaves daily and/or several double handfuls of Dandelion (Taraxacum Officinale) leaves, stems, flowers and roots as well if the horse will take them. Try the "taste test" with Garlic (dried granulated or freshly crushed by you) and Seaweed Meal. If the horse will take them they can be added to the feed.

If the condition is chronic the horse should also be treated professionally with a specially prescribed mixture of herbal extracts selected from Rosehips, Chamomile, Peppermint, Marshmallow, Meadowsweet, Aloes, Yarrow, Comfrey, Dandelion, Agrimony and Garlic. Bach Flower essences such as Oak, Impatiens, Crab Apple and Gentian would be also be included.

Chronic scouring will usually take at least 3 months to rectify, sometimes up to 8 months before completely normal droppings are achieved. As the droppings improve considerably indicating that the function of the gut is returning to normal, herbal extracts may be replaced with a dried herb mixture added to the feed for the remainder of the period of treatment. After this a careful natural feeding and supplements program needs to be maintained as quite often any little changes can cause a regression.

THE LIVER

The liver is the largest gland in the body and is an important organ of the digestive system, but it is vitally concerned directly or indirectly in all bodily functions. Therefore hepatic herbs are always necessary if a horse is in ill health, especially in the digestive system. They are also indicated as a tonic aid to improving general health. There are a variety of herbs which can be used depending upon the individual - Dandelion, Agrimony, Yellow Dock, St Marys Thistle, Fenugreek and Gentian.

Dandelion is the choice as a tonic aid to general health with many added benefits. St Marys Thistle and Gentian are indicated where there is heavier detoxification work to be done or where there is liver damage. Agrimony and Yellow Dock are quite similar and also work on kidneys and spleen.

The liver is the powerhouse of the body receiving blood rich in digested foods which it metabolises into cell nutrients. As the horse does not have a gall bladder like humans do, the liver is solely responsible for secreting bile to initiate digestion in the gut. The liver also plays the vital role of cleansing the blood of toxins such as drugs and poisons. It has the amazing ability to regenerate itself and hepatic herbs stimulate and support this vitally important activity. Liver damage is caused by toxins, poisons, long term drug use, viral and bacterial infections and migrating worm larvae.

APPETITE AND FEED CONVERSION

Horses with "picky" or poor appetites usually have poor feed conversion rates, but horses with huge appetites can also have the same problem. The first thing to do is to be sure that these horses are not carrying worm burdens. Very often these horses are receiving an inappropriate diet high in processed feeds. Feed conversion and appetite can be normalised with the provision of a natural feeding and supplements program in conjunction with a 12 week course of prescribed herbal treatments.

One of the best herbs to improve appetite and feed conversion in conjunction with the right diet for the horse in question is Fenugreek. The Greek horsemen fed their horses Fenugreek hay. The herb is better known to us as an ingredient in curry powders! It has quite a high oestrogen content so is contra-indicated for use in mares who have or are suspected of having imbalanced hormones.

Pancreatic function is intimately concerned with appetite and feed conversion and if this needs stimulation in either direction Fennel may be indicated as part of a mixture to balance appetite and feed conversion.

If a horse suddenly drops a lot of weight even though the appetite and food intake are normal, expert veterinary attention should immediately be sought.

Horses which are overweight and "live on the smell of an oil rag" are usually ponies or plain or cross bred horses which have the ability to do very well. These horses only need very plain feeding. See Laminitis.

If however a horse is particularly obese, there can be a number of other reasons such as an under active thyroid and expert veterinary attention should be sought to establish the cause. Once this is done herbs can often be used for rebalancing but this is an area where blood tests are necessary.

14 THE MUSCULO-SKELETAL SYSTEM

The musculo-skeletal system is the one that causes the most headaches to horse owners. All manner of problems manifest here as symptoms in varying degrees of severity, but the causes are very often to be found elsewhere in the body and from external influences.

LAMENESS

If a horse is even mildly lame, there is a reason. Pain is nature's way of telling a body to rest and heal. Just giving the horse bute and a few days off or worse still bute and no time off, is not going to solve the problem. More than likely it will make it worse. Finding out why a horse is lame can be a frustrating business. But we have to give it our best shot, so that appropriate treatment can be found. A specialist equine vet whose opinion you trust is the best person to diagnose in matters of severe or continuing lameness. Usually if a lameness is mild you can find a reason yourself - heat or swelling in a leg indicating a minor strain or sprain, stone bruise, abscess brewing, infection or shoeing problem. You can then administer appropriate practical and herbal first aid. The main thing is to take action as soon as you notice something is wrong. Don't leave it in the hope it will go away! On the other hand there is no point in flying into a panic and phoning the vet every time a horse has a minor problem which you can learn to deal with effectively yourself.

MUSCLES

Although it is impossible to separate out muscles from bones, tendons and ligaments, as they are all connected by the fascia, we will look first at the muscular system. The word fascia simply means bandage. It is a sheet of fibrous connective tissue, deep in the skin, that covers, supports and separates muscles and other organs. If the skeleton was removed there would still be a standing shape composed of fascia, muscles, tendons and ligaments - a kind of rubbery figure!

If there is spasm or actual fibre damage anywhere in the fascia it effectively strangles the muscle, severely inhibiting circulation, which means nutrients are not coming in and wastes are not going out the way they should.

There are a variety of muscle therapists who work on horses using different techniques - for example Equine Muscle Release Therapy (Bowen for horses). In my experience E.M.R.T. when carried out by a qualified practitioner is remarkably effective and combined with my herbal treatments produces excellent synergistic results.

Regardless of the technique a well trained therapist who is experienced in treating horses can be of great assistance in relieving symptoms, especially in association with herbal remedies. There are a number of herbs which are anti-spasmodic in their action - Chamomile, Valerian and Black Cohosh - to name a few, which if chosen and used appropriately will be of great benefit.

The trick is to establish and treat the cause of the problem as well. Causes include bio-mechanical imbalance (often the result of poor shoeing, dentistry and/or saddle fit), unbalanced riders, over-acidity, inappropriate training and feeding.

Over acidity is a major cause of general muscle tightness and soreness as well as the occurrence of muscle spasm. Many horses show these symptoms without actually tying-up. Tight hamstring muscles, short stepping behind, girthiness, general aversion to being touched and crankiness are all indicators. Natural feeding of generous amounts of roughage and limiting protein and grain intake is the key to treatment and prevention together with herbal treatment to remove acid, balance hydration and assist kidney function. Herbs such as Celery, Juniper, Dandelion and Valerian are specific for balancing pH in the body of the horse.

AZOTURIA (TYING-UP)

Symptoms vary from a slight stiffness in the hind quarter through to a total reluctance to move with sweating and obvious pain. Damage, in varying degrees, is caused to muscle cells as lactic acid is released causing muscle cramps. If cell damage is severe the urine will be dark coloured. In very severe cases kidney damage can occur, occasionally being irreparable.

The condition can often occur after a day off especially with fit horses getting a lot of grain, but also occurs in unfit horses which are worked too hard or too long or who become stressed. Horses (often mares) with a nervous disposition are more prone to tying-up.

Some horses recover completely from an attack and never suffer from it again, whereas others develop a chronic condition with worsening attacks.

If tying-up is suspected immediately STOP WORK. Trying to continue work even in mild cases will cause further damage to the muscles. Immediately administer Rescue Remedy. During summer, cool the horse down by hosing. In cold weather, keep the horse warm with suitable rugs. Drench with

200ml Rosehips tea and 200ml Celery seed tea (for an average sized horse). Rosehips is incredibly high in Vitamin C which is specific for stress. Celery is a natural diuretic, encourages the horse to drink and urinate and is acid removing. Prompt treatment promotes a quicker recovery and helps to prevent further attacks. In mild cases encourage the horse to self exercise by turning out in a grassy paddock.

In severe cases when the horse is virtually seized up, give Rescue Remedy, immediately call your vet who will probably administer non-steroidal anti-inflammatory drugs or Aspirin. This will alleviate symptoms. Herbal alternatives are Devil's Claw or White Willow in the extract form which can also be used as follow-up treatment. Rescue Remedy and Rosehips tea should continue to be given at hourly intervals for severe cases and three times daily for mild cases. Dehydration often results from a bad attack and natural electrolytes can be provided by syringing Dandelion extract diluted in water straight into the mouth. Dosage rate would vary from 2ml to 10ml depending on the size of the horse and the degree of dehydration.

Management is very important in the prevention of tying-up. Firstly reduce the energy / protein feed intake on days off : always warm the horse up and cool it down properly: do not work the horse hard for a whole session, have a few walk intervals : and build the horse's fitness level / work level gradually. Walking is the ideal way to warm up but it takes 20 minutes at the walk to warm the muscles through. Cooling down at the walk usually takes about 10 minutes depending upon the weather and the horse's degree of fitness.

Horses prone to tying-up should not be fed bran as a substance in it called phytate apparently inhibits calcium metabolism. Provide free access to a lump of natural rock salt, feed 1 tablespoon high grade dolomite twice daily, 1 tablespoon Australian seaweed meal twice daily and give 50ml of apple cider vinegar daily diluted in water to dampen

down the feed (for an average sized horse of 450kg/990lb).
This ensures adequate supply of the minerals potassium,
sodium and calcium which are important in preventing
Azoturia. Another mineral thought to assist is Selenium which
is found in seaweed and garlic. Vitamin E is also thought to
assist and this is found in black sunflower seeds.

To provide enough energy and protein feeds for
performance horses that are prone to acidity or actual tying-
up, feed corn oil, whole barley which has been simmered for
an hour to break open the husks, black sunflower seeds and
cold pressed linseed oil or boiled linseeds. It is easy to make a
porridge with 1 teacup (250ml/8½fl oz) french white millet
and ½ cup whole linseeds as a daily ration for an average sized
horse.

Tying-up is a condition which usually
responds well to appropriate herbal treatment
combined with the correct management and
diet. It is a common condition which I treat and
professional help should be sought to prevent
recurrence.

MUSCLE WASTAGE

"Muscles control movement of the body. They are attached
to bone via tendons. An adequate and blood nerve supply is
essential for normal function. Muscle wastage (atrophy) is
either due to lack of use or due to damage to the nerve supply.
The site of muscle atrophy does not necessarily imply that the
problem is in that area." (6)

The cause of muscle wastage must be identified and
rectified if normal muscle bulk is to be returned.
A combination of prescribed herbal mixtures and muscle
therapy can be an excellent option for treatment. One of the
muscle building herbs Saw Palmetto, which is a natural steroid
or Oats, in the extract form as opposed to the feed form are

always indicated. Care must be taken in the use of Saw Palmetto as it can be make some geldings behave like stallions and it is not usually an option for use in mares. Circulatory herbs to use in conjunction include Fenugreek, Violet, Nettles, Rue, Hawthorn and Rosehips while detoxification herbs are also important in this equation.

Muscle wastage may be very obvious or it may only be detected by the eye of an expert.

HOW TO CHECK YOUR OWN HORSE

Stand him up on level ground very square. Stand behind him and look over the whole rump area - look for the symmetry or asymmetry of the muscles on the top, sides and down the legs.

From the same position stand on a crate so you are higher and check the muscles either side of the back and wither and along the neck to the poll.

Stand in front and feel the muscles on either side of the neck just behind the ears - still looking for symmetry or asymmetry.

Check the bite alignment of the teeth - they should not be overshot or undershot and most horses who are accused of this actually have their jaws out of alignment due to faulty (or no) horse dentistry.

Ride your horse in walk, trot and canter in a straight line on a firm to hard, even surface and listen carefully - the beat should be even - four for walk, two for trot and three for canter. If not - you have a bio-mechanical problem which needs fixing.

Last but not least, if you really feel you just can't bend your horse properly no matter what you do, you are very likely right. If you are balanced and straight, it should be relatively easy, IF your horse can physically do what you are asking of him. IF NOT, he needs therapy.

Look at the horse's front feet - one may be smaller than the other. This is because the horse is loading that shoulder and is stabbing the ground with that foot and not opening the frog to get the circulation going properly. When he is balanced, over a period of 2-3 months that foot should become identical to the other.

Muscle tissue takes much longer to regenerate than most other body tissues and needs appropriate exercise to rebuild mass. This is also one time when additional protein may need to be added to the diet. Soybean meal as well as black sunflower seeds may be called for depending on the individual and the degree of damage.

THE SKELETON - BONES, TENDONS AND LIGAMENTS

The conventional view of lameness is that 70% is in the forelimb and probably in the foot. Whilst this is true as regards symptoms, the causes are to be found elsewhere in the musculo-skeletal system.

If a foot is constantly striking the ground incorrectly this will set up other pathologies, so if a limb and foot are stressed for long enough a problem will be set up whereby you have an actual bone disease. Basically it is a repetitive strain injury. The forces must go up through the shock absorber system and be absorbed by the body. If they don't you are going to have big problems due to a bio-mechanical malfunction.

The other predisposing factors to bone diseases of the foot and lower leg are genetics, poor conformation, mineral deficiencies, poor shoeing, incorrect feeding, imbalances in other body systems and all the causes of muscular problems already mentioned.

ARTHRITIS

Also known as Osteo-Arthritis or Degenerative Joint Disease, this is one of the most common afflictions of man and horse. There are countless remedies for this virtually incurable condition. My professionally prescribed herbal treatments and natural diet are successful in alleviating symptoms and staving off further degeneration. However it is a condition which requires maintenance treatment. Mitigating the effects of stiffness and pain allows many horses to continue in work or makes retired horses more comfortable and more mobile, which assists further in keeping the disease at bay until the horse is a lot older. Obviously the earlier the condition is recognised and treated, the better, because in the earlier stages cartilage can be favourably influenced to regenerate.

The herbs I select from to treat arthritis include Celery, Juniper, Chamomile, Horsetail, Guaiacum, Devil's Claw , Burdock, Tansy and Comfrey. But as with all holistic forms of treatment the state of all the other body systems is also taken into account and concurrently balanced for best results.

Management of arthritis horses is important. They are always worse in the winter or in cold weather so suitable rugging is essential to keep them warm. Sheepskin lined suede paddock boots are also an excellent option for some horses.

External treatment is the sparing use of a combination of oils - 50% Comfrey, 50% Linseed, 5% Arnica and 1% Wintergreen. Care must be taken when using these oils, especially Wintergreen because of its blistering qualities. The Wintergreen penetrates deeply into tissue including the bones of the foot carrying the benefits of the other oils with it - Comfrey for healing, Arnica for bruising and Linseed for retensioning ligaments and tendons.

A completely natural feeding and supplements program is essential to the treatment of arthritis. The dangers of an over-acid producing diet are discussed fully in the chapter Are You Feeding Against Yourself? Essential supplements in a diet to prevent and treat arthritis are high grade dolomite, Australian seaweed, apple cider vinegar, cold pressed linseed oil or cod liver oil, Garlic, Chamomile and free access to rock salt.

PREVENTION IS THE WAY

Prevention is of course the answer. The number of horses suffering from arthritis even at a young age is quite staggering. This can be prevented with good diet, herbs and training. Recent data from the USA showed that every one of a group of 36 horses that had been euthanased at the racetrack from two year olds through to nine year olds had the beginnings of arthritis in the spine. (Source Dr Ian Bidstrup)

Dr Bidstrup is an Australian veterinarian who specialises exclusively in equine chiropractic and acupuncture. He has this message for horse owners and managers. "Movement is health and that means appropriate lateral and dorsal flexion of the spine. Inappropriate early training will inevitably lead to arthritis. From a chiropractic point of view joint damage in the limbs is often a result of body imbalance which causes greater stress to some joints with resulting wear and tear and breakdown of the affected joints."

There are an increasing number of veterinarians who are trained in equine chiropractic and acupuncture, many of whom are members of the Australian Holistic Veterinary Association.

If you are considering chiropractic or acupuncture as part of a natural therapy program for your horses, it is highly recommended that professional help be sought from veterinarians who are trained in these modalities. Horse chiropractors who are not trained in equine physiology and anatomy can do more harm than good. A graphic example of this is the common practice of pulling limbs way out of the normal range of motion.

The correct first aid and follow up treatment of horses for

trauma or injury, especially involving bones, which would possibly be a site for future arthritic degeneration is an essential arthritic preventative measure. First aid measures include dosing with Rescue Remedy, homeopathic Arnica and Rosehips tea. It is essential that horses receive appropriate mineral supplementation when they are undergoing healing, as it is at all times. Follow up treatment to prevent arthritis involves herbal treatments to assist the body to complete the healing process especially in the area of tissue regeneration and detoxification, a natural feeding and supplements program, adequate spelling and management followed by structured return to work programs.

There are many names for arthritis and bone conditions in different parts of the skeletal system - such as Navicular, Ringbone, Sidebone, Bone Spavin, Pedalosteitis, Sesamoiditis, chips and spurs. From a naturopathic point of view they are all similar in that they are part of a body system that is going wrong, so herbal treatment, whilst it must be differential, involves selection from the group of herbs already mentioned. As with any condition, holistic herbal treatment combined with other natural therapies and sound management to treat the symptoms and the underlying causes is essential. Natural diet can easily be implemented by owners but professional help should be sought for best results to further improve bone conditions including arthritis.

SPLINTS

Splints are caused by trauma to the periosteum (the covering of the bone) either by outside injury or by stresses placed on the leg from inappropriate work, poor conformation and mineral deficiencies.

The first thing to do when a horse "throws a splint" is to apply first aid in the form of ice packs, followed by the application of Arnica ointment and pressure bandaging

(provided you are competent to do this correctly as I have seen
horses have their tendons bowed by too tight bandaging
without proper pads underneath the bandage). If the skin is
broken use Witch Hazel lotion or ointment instead of the
Arnica. Either of these are to mitigate the effects of bruising.
Internally homeopathic Arnica 6C and Rescue Remedy should
also be given. If the splint is reactive to pressure and/or the
horse is lame, seek immediate advice from a specialist equine
vet who will x-ray to make sure there is no fracture of the
splint bone and who will advise on the amount of time the
horse should be spelled to allow healing. This will also depend
on the position of the splint. Some splints will never cause a
soundness problem whereas others will if not dealt with
properly in the first instance. The first aid treatment above is
good for the first few days. After that sparing amounts of
Comfrey oil or ointment or poultice should be applied daily.
Old splints - unless you want to show the horse leave them
alone, but if you want to try to reduce the size, massage Castor
Oil into the splint for a few minutes daily. If there is any sign
of blistering, immediately cease and re-start every second day.
It will take 6-12 weeks to work and may not in all cases.
There are lots of remedies - old and new for splints. Adequate
mineral intake in utero, as a young horse and throughout life is
the best prevention.

TENDONS AND LIGAMENTS

Damaged tendons and ligaments require an accurate
diagnosis by an experienced equine vet, using ultrasound
equipment, who will advise the amount of time the horse
needs to be spelled to affect complete healing. The rate and
quality of healing can be accelerated by the use of prescribed
internal and external herbal treatments.

External treatment by daily massaging with Raw Linseed
Oil to help retension tendons and ligaments is indicated once

inflammation has subsided. Comfrey Oil can be added for its healing properties. Some horses blister easily with repeated applications of oils, so use sparingly and if there is any sign of blistering, stop for a few days and re-start every second day.

The big three herbs to use internally for tendon and ligament healing are Comfrey, Yarrow, Devil's Claw together with boiled linseeds and millet in the diet. Detoxifying and circulatory herbs are often needed as well. If there is any concern of infection in a tendon sheath, Comfrey should be replaced with antiseptic and blood cleansing herbs.

Patella lock is quite a common condition which results in the horse being unable to adopt normal flexion of the hind leg or legs affected. Massaging raw linseed oil into the front of the stifle joint at the site of the medial ligament may help to retension it, if you persevere for long enough. Prescribed internal herbal treatment has also been seen to benefit the condition which can be so severe that the horse can seize up for short periods of time.

Good management and diet is essential over spelling and healing periods. Always have your vet check that the healing has gone according to plan before bringing the horse back into work.

AVOIDING BREAKDOWN

"Breakdowns have generally been chalked up to the failure of normal bone under abnormal circumstances (the "bad step" on the track) : in fact, bone scans make it clear that these are mostly failures of abnormal bone under normal circumstances. The most frequent sites of breakdown - the humerus, cannon bones, sesamoids, and fetlocks - are precisely the same places where stress fractures or weakening is observed in bone scans of lame, and even many sound racehorses." (2)

The natural diet, avoiding drugs with known side effects which weaken bone together with early spelling and herbal treatment of all musculo-skeletal problems is the best way to prevent breakdowns.

RETURN TO WORK PROGRAMS

Structured return to work programs are an essential part of the healing process. The following program forms the foundation for an interval training program used by many event riders and has been designed by Andrew McLean, EFA/NCAS Level 2 Eventing Instructor and winner of the prestigious Gawler Three Day Event. I have used and recommended this program successfully. It is ideal to bring horses back into work after injury to tendons, ligaments or bones, or after illness. It is based on the idea that bone, tendon and ligament respond to concussive stress by growing denser.

Bone is dynamic tissue, it is constantly growing and remodelling and it is important to strengthen it and associated tissues such as ligaments and tendons correctly so that the horse will remain sound and fit. All horses need periods of work on hard, firm surfaces to do this. Constant work on soft, deep surfaces such as dressage arenas will not in itself strengthen bone, ligament and tendon tissue and in fact can lead to leg problems as bones etc. becomes less dense.

The program takes six weeks. It consists of progressive, long, slow distance work to increase density of bone, tendon and ligament. This is not a fittening aspect, it is simply to make the chassis of the horse strong enough to continue usefully in its own sport, whatever it may be. This is the most essential aspect to prevent any problems.

Week One - Walking only 20-30 minutes on firm to hard, level surfaces, straight or slightly curved lines only - no circles. Only short breaks.

Week Two - Introduce short periods of trotting - 20-30

minutes on firm to hard, level surfaces. Say half trotting, half walking but trotting for only 5 minutes at a time. Straight or slightly curved lines only - no circles. Only short breaks.

Week Three - Long, slow distance work as above twice in the week, with one day off and on the other three/four days introduce dressage training work. Keep circles at least 20 metres in diameter, bigger if possible. Total time of work in this week 30 minutes.

Week Four through to Week Six - The same as for Week Three but the time gradually increases from 30 minutes to 1 hour. The dressage training also increases in intensity over these weeks. Canter is introduced in Week Four, short periods in the same manner as trot was introduced to the walk sessions. Circles no smaller than 15 metres.

If there is any sign of soreness, heat or swelling, at any stage, use cold hosing or ice pack therapy, give the horse 3-4 days off. If it is necessary to give the horse this time off, recommence the program at the point at which you left off. If it is necessary to give it longer, go back further and re-introduce herbal treatments. Using this program you will ensure that your horse has the toughness of bone, tendon and ligament that will help prevent work related injuries from occurring.

15 EXTERIOR GLOW = INNER HEALTH

A horse with a magnificent, rich, shining coat is a horse that is reflecting his inner and overall health. We are what we eat. No amount of shampoos, shiners and conditioners can create a brilliant coat, although they do make it clean and more beautiful.

The skin, hair and hooves make up the integumentary system and their condition is the barometer of good health or the lack of it. So if any of these are off in any way, you need to take action. All skin conditions, even those with external causes, such as parasites, are an indication of imbalances on the inside. Hooves have been covered in the chapter No Foot No Horse, so in this chapter we will talk about skin and hair.

Summer and winter both bring their share of seasonal difficulties which afflict skin and hair. In summer we have to contend with flies, mosquitoes, sunburn, itches, the effects of heat, ticks and so on. Winter is more the season for greasy heel and hoof problems.

QUEENSLAND (SWEET) ITCH

This condition, also known as Sweet Itch, is caused by an allergic reaction to bites from midges which is why some horses get the itch and others don't. It can be a very difficult condition to clear up permanently and requires great perseverance. Typically the afflicted horse rubs the hair out on mane, tail, forelock, ears and face. It can rub itself till it is raw or bleeding and infected sores are a secondary problem. Similar symptoms are also caused by other allergies and other skin parasites.

Treatment involves a four pronged approach - physical protection, external remedies, internal protection and treatment including diet.

Physical protection from bites includes rugging, repellents and if possible stabling at peak biting times of the day which is dawn and dusk. White, pure cotton combo rugs with generous tail flaps are the safest and best for paddock use. However they are easily ripped by scratching. Anything but pure white cotton is usually too hot in the summer causing the horse to sweat and making the skin more uncomfortable. A flyveil completes the protection. Hoods with ears sewn certainly keep the midges away but in a paddock situation, hoods are dangerous, as they can easily come over the eyes, causing a horse to damage itself in a fence. A recipe for herbal insect repellent can be found in First Aid. However this cannot be applied to areas where the skin is broken as it would cause stinging and possible irritation. The horse's skin should be kept as clean as possible by regular washing using Absorbine shampoo and conditioner for the mane and tail. To soothe and promote healing on the bald areas or where the skin is broken, sparingly apply Hypericum Oil on a regular basis. A rinse made from Chamomile and/or Calendula tea and/or fresh Aloe Vera gel direct from the plant is also soothing and healing to damaged skin. I often prescribe a dilute wash made from Calendula and Golden Seal extracts to which has been added the Bach flower essences Crab Apple and Rescue Remedy for many skin conditions.

Internal protection can be achieved to a certain extent by making the blood unpalatable to biting insects by routinely feeding Garlic. One tablespoon freshly crushed or dried granulated twice daily for the average sized horse. Keep sweet feeds such as molasses to a minimal or nil level as it tends to make the blood more palatable.

A completely natural feeding and supplements regime as outlined in the feeding chapters is an absolutely essential part of healing this condition. Do not feed any oils or oil based feeds except those recommended in the feeding chapters as they may be contra-indicated for skin conditions.

Prescribed herbal mixtures to be given for a full blood cycle (12 weeks) completes the treatment. I always formulate these according to the individual and the herbs I select from include Aloes, Chamomile, Devil's Claw, Euphorbia, Echinacea, Fenugreek, Garlic, Liquorice, Rosehips and Vervain. Bach flower essences usually include Beech, Impatiens, Rescue Remedy and Vervain.

TICKS

To reduce the number of ticks attaching to horses, keep the blood unpalatable as outlined above and ensure the general health of the horse is very good with the natural diet.

For external protection use Wormwood tea. This is a very bitter herb which if made into a strong tea and applied externally to the legs, face and belly of the horse in particular (do not get it in the eyes) will greatly reduce the numbers of ticks attaching. It has to be applied generously on a daily basis. Fresh Aloe Vera gel is good for soothing tick bites and Calendula tea, 10% extract wash or ointment should also be used for its antiseptic quality. Horses which have been habitually treated with chemicals to repel ticks should be treated with a liver detoxification treatment for 12 weeks.

SUNBURN

Horses with pink skin, white noses and white sox are much more prone to sunburn and one of the best ways of protecting them is to apply Zinc cream to the white areas on a daily basis taking care not to get it in their eyes or inside the nostrils. All horses, these ones in particular, should be able to access shady trees or shelters in the heat of the day.

GREASY HEEL (MUD FEVER)

This is a fungal condition which can be permanently cleared up with a combination of natural diet and external herbal treatment. Particularly chronic cases may also need prescribed internal herbal mixtures, as Greasy Heel can lead to Cellulitis which is more serious. Horses prone to greasy heel are usually not receiving enough copper in their diet.
They should be put on the natural diet including generous quantities of Rosehips. To remove the scabs without having to pull them off, which is extremely painful for the horse, first wash the affected areas with herbal shampoo, rinse thoroughly and pat dry with a clean towel. Then apply Thuja ointment. The best way is to make up your own ointment using Sorbolene cream as the base and stirring in 5% Thuja extract. Then apply cling wrap, a pad to keep it in place and bandage for 24 hours. The scabs will come away easily.
This process may need to be repeated for several days depending on how bad the Greasy Heel is, but once all the scabs are off, you can just wash and apply the ointment, without the bandaging until the condition clears. If you do this and maintain the natural diet, the condition should not return.
Calendula Ointment can then be used to grow hair back and reduce scarring.

LICE

Once again the natural diet is essential, especially for the provision of sufficient sulphur and copper to prevent lice. However to treat horses afflicted with Lice, use sulphur dusting powder along the top and back of the horse, through the legs, the top of the tail and through the mane. Repeat the treatment in 10 days to remove the newly hatched nits. Rugs should also be cleansed at the same time using sulphur and straight apple cider vinegar to remove nits. Good management, diet and hygiene should prevent the occurrence of Lice.

MANGE

Mange is caused by a parasitic, microscopic Mite. Itchy, inflamed skin lesions will result usually on the head and neck or legs so the horse will scratch badly causing hair loss. Mange is easily transferred between horses and on saddlery and equipment. Wormwood tea or a decoction made from Garlic, lemons and apple cider vinegar can be used to treat the condition externally. Natural diet, good management and hygiene is a preventative.

RINGWORM

This is a highly contagious fungal condition. Horses can be infected from other animals, tack, grooming gear or from stables, fences and vehicles. Humans may catch ringworm from horses. Young horses and horses receiving insufficient copper in their diet are particularly susceptible and the condition is easily contracted at breaking-in yards and stables. Ringworms are usually found on the head, girth and saddle area. They are not itchy but the hair falls out and the skin is scaly underneath. The horse should be isolated, all gear and tack to which it has been exposed should be disinfected. Add 10 drops each of concentrated Thyme Oil and Pine Oil to 5 litres (UK 8¾pt; US 11pt) of water to make a disinfectant to use on gear and tack.

The affected areas on the horse should be treated externally twice daily with Thuja ointment. Or make a decoction from garlic and lemons and add apple cider vinegar after it is cooled and strained. The natural diet, good management and hygiene is a preventative.

WARTS

Warts are viral in origin. In young horses Warts (also known as milk warts) will appear often around the muzzle and usually spontaneously disappear within a couple of months.

Another type of Wart is one which appears singly anywhere on the body without causing any problems if not damaged. These can grow larger or smaller or disappear.

Warts can become a problem if they are situated in places where they may be caused to bleed by rugs or tack. Externally Thuja ointment is effective against Warts, but it must remain in contact with them all the time so has to be applied several times daily over a few months. Homeopathic Thuja given internally is a more practical option

SARCOIDS

Sarcoids are also thought to be caused by a virus and can become very large and multiple. They can be defeated, especially in the earlier stages, using Thuja ointment combined with the natural diet and internal herbal treatment to stimulate the immune and lymphatic systems and provide anti-biotic and anti-tumour action. Professional assistance is needed to formulate a mixture. If they are removed surgically either conventionally or by laser beam they will often return, so an internal herbal mixture with the same objectives as for treatment is advisable for prevention.

ALLERGIC REACTIONS ON THE SKIN

Dermatitis is an inflammatory condition of the skin that may be caused by an external influence which has set up the irritation. Usual causes are hair dyes, shampoos, insect repellents, coat shine products and soap powders that have been used to wash rugs and saddle cloths. Some horses have particularly sensitive skins and products containing chemicals should be avoided. I always use and recommend pure herbal shampoo which contains no sodium or ammonium laureth. For conditioning manes and tails, also use a pure herbal conditioner. Only use show-shine products on tails. A liquid wool wash containing Eucalyptus is good for rugs and saddle cloths and Napisan can be used as a safe whitener.

Allergic reactions on the skin like lumps, welts, fluid filled swellings can have myriad causes. They can be from bites, feed or bedding, chemicals either ingested or used externally, from the Onchocerca worm or an allergy to almost anything in the environment. Causes are often undiscovered but an attempt must be made to do so, so it can be removed if at all possible. Acute and severe reactions should be dealt with by your vet who will most likely administer a single Cortisone injection. See chapter Herbal Alternatives to Drugs. After this or in the first instance for less severe reactions, Chamomile Tea and Rescue Remedy should be given internally at regular intervals and can also be used to soothe externally as a compress. Fresh Aloe Vera gel is also useful for bites.

Professional help should be sought for internal herbal treatment which always involves other body systems, such as the immune, blood and circulatory, liver and kidneys. Just using skin herbs is rarely the answer for skin conditions and treatment varies considerably from horse to horse.

TUMOURS

Grey horses are extremely susceptible to Melanomas, even though many grey horses with huge growths on them live to a ripe old age. It is highly advisable to seek a veterinary diagnosis if you suspect a tumour, to find out if it is malignant or benign.

There are many herbs which have anti-tumour and anti-cancerous properties - Comfrey, Garlic, Red Clover, Rosehips and Violet. Antiseptic, immuno-stimulants and lymphatic cleansing herbs are also indicated. Professional advice must be sought for herbal treatment in this area.

COAT CONDITION

If the coat is dull, dry, scurfy or pale in colour, this is an indication of inadequate nutrition especially in relation to minerals and imbalances in other body systems. The natural diet and a course of appropriate herbs usually brings about obvious changes in a few weeks with a shiny, clear, rich coloured coat resulting within 2-3 months.

16 THE IMMUNE SYSTEM AND VIRUSES

The natural immunity of a body, be it man or horse, is a precious possession which requires care, not abuse. Feeding concentrated chemicalised feeds, constantly injecting drugs and manufactured vitamins constitutes abuse which seriously weakens the immune system. In today's world, a healthy immune system is the best protection any horse can have from the nasty array of pathogens that are constantly mutating and resistant to commercial antibiotics. Happily there are many common herbs which are deceptively powerful in stimulating the immune system and treating infections and viruses.

VIRUSES

There are no antibiotic drugs which are effective against viruses and vaccines never produce 100% protection.

Australia is free of many of the world's equine viral diseases, especially notable being equine flu. Let's hope we are still free of it post Olympic Games as there is no way that the quarantine authorities can be 100% sure that equine influenza was not in the visiting Olympic horses.

"The most common viral diseases of horses are cold viruses. Most young horses go through a string of viral colds just like children do. Often the only symptom is a watery nasal discharge and an intermittent cough. If bacteria take the opportunity to multiply in the tissues damaged by the viruses then we may get problems such as snotty noses, abscessing glands between the lower jaws (like that of Strangles) and/or bacterial pneumonia. Equine Herpes Virus Type 4 (EHV4) is a particularly troublesome bug in that it often causes a cough that recurs as soon as the horse resumes exercise and is more likely to be associated with abscessed glands and pneumonia than most of the common cold viruses. Other common and troublesome viral diseases are equine coital exanthema (a mild venereal disease) and Ross River Fever which causes lameness and swelling of joints, and at times poor performance and dullness, and rotavirus which causes scouring in foals. Equine Herpes Viral Abortion (EHV1) is uncommon but can cause abortion storms. It has also been associated with hind limb inco-ordination and paralysis. Herpes viruses by nature are latent viruses, meaning that they can lay in hiding and then, when the animal is stressed, become active again. This is blamed for poor performance in some cases and in particular the recurrence of an annoying cough. Ross River Fever virus infections are implicated in many cases where the horse has been through a period of malaise, lameness and joint swelling which passes but then does not seem all that well for some time." (9)

A good natural diet employing herbal preventive health nutrition is the best way to prevent viruses. Herbal medicinal treatments are particularly effective in resolving viruses and post-viral syndrome. The course of treatment must be undertaken continuously over one full blood cycle (12 weeks) using Garlic and Echinacea. The herb Red Clover is specific especially where joints are effected and other herbs selected will depend upon the particular virus. If it has attacked the respiratory system the herb Elecampagne is used to lift wastes out of the lungs. If the virus has attacked the joints there are many herbs which can assist to relieve the stiffness and to cleanse the blood including Horsetail, Guaiacum, Burdock, Tansy, Nettles and Rue. In addition the liver will always be supported in its vital detoxification role with the use of herbs such as Agrimony, Dandelion or St Marys Thistle.

Horses can become very depressed and lethargic when suffering from a virus or post-viral syndrome. The Bach flower essences Gorse, Hornbeam, Olive, Oak, Sweet Chestnut, Wild Rose along with the old faithful Rescue Remedy are chosen from and added to the herbs, to lift a horse's spirits which in turn greatly assists fight back.

TRAVEL SICKNESS

One of the major causes of travel sickness is an already weakened immune system with the added ingredient of stress.

We all know how stressful moving house can be. Well it's no different for a horse! Horses travelling to a new home or to a competition often experience stress. It is extremely important to avoid or fix this common problem. It can lead to travel sickness and definitely impairs performance of horse and rider.

Travel sickness can prove fatal. Symptoms include some or all of the following - elevated temperature, colic, stiffness in limbs, dehydration, not eating or drinking, lethargy, respiratory distress. Three serious complications are pneumonia, stress founder and impaired liver function.

Stress is brought about by horses being travelled for too long a distance at a time, especially in hot weather, insufficient rests, not drinking, poor ventilation, bad driving, poorly designed floats (trailers or horse boxes), inadequate care and horses who travel badly. The horse who already has a weakened immune system is particularly susceptible to picking up an infection en route.

To help prevent travel stress or sickness ensure horses' immune systems are in optimum condition. The natural diet including routine feeding of Garlic, Rosehips and apple cider vinegar as preventive nutrition is the first step. Secondly any horses which have been affected by infection, especially respiratory or viral problems, should be treated for one full blood cycle (12 weeks) preferably at onset, to provide blood cleansing and immune system stimulation. This is the best bet to prevent the problem from returning at a later date as herbs assist the body to heal itself, they don't just remove symptoms.

Previous infections have a nasty habit of returning at times of "peak fitness" if they have not been completely healed in the first place. Absence of symptoms does not equal cure. Healing goes on unseen in the body for long periods of time after symptoms have gone. Herbs stimulate the body to complete the healing process.

For horses travelling to an important race or competition, individualised herbal mixtures can be formulated and given for 10 days or so prior to travel, during the event and return travel and for a few days after arriving home.

A general herbal preventative for travel stress can be given in the form of Rosehips and Chamomile Teas with the Bach Flower essence Rescue Remedy for a few days before, during and after travel. For an average sized horse, once daily, 1 tablespoon Rosehips granules and 2 tablespoons flowers of Chamomile made into a tea together with 500ml (17½fl oz) boiling water. Allow to steep for 15 minutes. Add 4 drops of Rescue Remedy to 60ml of the cooled tea and syringe over the tongue. Put the rest in the feed including the dregs.

For horses that are bad travellers give Rescue Remedy prior to them realising they are going somewhere in the float and this can be repeated a few times daily or hourly if necessary while travelling and at a show.

If travel stress or sickness is suspected the horse must be immediately spelled and veterinary attention sought. Herbal treatment can be used in association with veterinary treatment. Specific herbal treatment should continue for one full blood cycle for the reasons outlined above.

Drinking is essential during travel to prevent dehydration. Some horses drink no matter what, others are very fussy. It is a good idea to get fussy horses used to drinking molasses water so that different water can be disguised when travelling. Get into the habit of offering these horses molasses water after work diluted at the rate of 1 tablespoon to 5 litres (UK 8¾pt; US 11pt). A good remedy to encourage drinking is to make a tea from Celery Seeds (1 tablespoon to 500ml [17½fl oz] water) and give this as part of the daily feed until normal drinking

habits are established. Always allow horses
free access to a lump of natural rock salt in
their feeder and be sure to take this with you
when travelling.

Horses are taken to competitions, studs, trainers or new
properties all the time. A lot of energy and dollars are spent on
preparation for events. The same care and attention should be
expended on the travelling aspect. One bad trip can have
disastrous long term effects.

HEADSHAKING SYNDROME

This unexplained and vexing condition has been known for
over 100 years. I believe after treating quite a few Headshakers
successfully that it may be connected with a weakened
immune system with symptoms manifesting in the nervous
and upper respiratory systems.

The cause of the symptoms is apparently a severe
neuralgia in the nerves of the face but the cause of this nerve
pain is not known. The symptoms can be so severe that the
horse can damage himself and his handlers and has to be put
down. The typical symptoms of Headshaking Syndrome are
throwing the head violently up and down and/or to the side,
striking and stamping with the front legs, rubbing nostrils and
eyes against the legs or the nose along the ground, excessive
snorting. Often the ears are held stiffly out to the side as if the
horse is being annoyed by a bot fly. Some horses show these
symptoms only under saddle while others also show them on
the lunge or at liberty. The longer the horse is worked and the
hotter it gets, the worse the symptoms become. Having owned
a Headshaker myself I can testify to this and I have a broken
cheek bone to prove it! Every case history I know of is the
same in this respect. However some horses are worse on hot,
sunny days, others on cold, windy days. Many horses do not
show the symptoms if ridden when or where there is no

sunlight, hence it is sometimes termed photic headshaking. In some horses the condition only manifests in the spring and summer, subsiding in autumn and winter. A few are the opposite. In some horses the condition is with them all year round but it can spontaneously resolve only to return again, often years later. Headshaking can afflict all breeds, sexes and colours of horse.

Owners of Headshakers look for many ways to resolve the problem, usually without success. These include checking for ear mites, different bits, saddles, checking and adjusting saddle fit, change of feeds, change of environment, different training methods, change of sport, spelling, change of shoeing, dental, chiropractic, acupuncture and drug treatments. A treatment option which involves surgery is neurectomy, but as with all forms of treatment for headshaking, there is no guarantee of success.

Recent veterinary research has shown one cause to be an infection and inflammation of the inner ear which spreads to the bones that control tongue and voice box movement. This is a potentially fatal condition.

It is also thought that horses that have been exposed to the EHV1 virus are more at risk and this may be a trigger.

Some likely causes are allergies, light sensitivity and/or photo-sensitivity, Magnesium deficiency, spinal and/or cervical misalignment, teeth problems, ear mites, fungal rhinitis and periodic opthalmia.

I know of one successful treatment of an allergy caused case using hyposensitisation vaccines made by isotope tagging of the horse's blood.

Trying to find out the causes is extremely difficult. Other natural therapies which have proved successful in a few cases include homeopathy, veterinary chiropractic and acupuncture and Bach flower remedies.

17 BLOOD, CIRCULATION AND LYMPHATICS

Blood is an important barometer of health from both herbal and veterinary viewpoints. Whilst blood tests are a useful diagnostic tool, it should be understood that they are not conclusive. For example where there are slight variations above or below the accepted normal levels, these could change again if blood from the same horse was taken and retested in as little a time as 24 hours after the original test. A horse's liver or kidneys for example may be operating below par, but this may not show up on a blood test. Usually only a chronic imbalance will show up or when the point of actual disease has been reached.

The class of herbs known as alteratives, or blood cleansers, work on the blood to purify, removing infections or the remains of previous infections, causing elimination and healing processes. They are also used to detoxify the body of drug and chemical residues. There are also herbs which exert a beneficial influence over blood circulation and cleanse the lymphatic circulation which runs parallel to the blood circulation.

The herb Nettles is a marvellous aid for the treatment of anaemia, which is a condition of blood when the red cell count is too low. Red cells are responsible for the absorption and transport of oxygen from the lungs, transport via the bloodstream throughout the body and collection of carbon dioxide to take back to the lungs for expulsion. There are many causes of anaemia ranging from worm burdens, internal bleeding through to imbalances in other body systems such as liver and spleen and actual disease. The cause should be determined so that it can be treated along with the symptoms. Nettles are very high in Iron, also improve the quality of arterial blood flow and the activity of the spleen, especially in its role of removing warn out red blood cells. Red Clover is another herb which will raise the red cell count quickly as it is also high in Copper which is needed for absorption of Iron.

The common practice of feeding iron tonics routinely to prevent anaemia is without foundation as Australian soils are rich in Iron but deficient in Copper. So usually once adequate Copper is received by the horse in question, the anaemia will be resolved.

When the white cell count in blood is out of balance, showing a higher than normal count, this means the horse's immune system is under assault from pathogens. If the white cell count is low, the immune system is depressed and functioning below par. Echinacea is the herb of choice here and is renowned for its anti-viral, anti-bacterial and immuno-stimulant properties.

Nettles may often be prescribed with its metabolic partner Rue which balances the venous pressure with the arterial pressure and balances the viscosity and flow. Rue is very high in Rutin (Vitamins P) and Vitamin K supporting the clotting and anti-clotting substances of the blood. Nettles and Rue are used together in varying proportions where the circulation needs stimulation, such as in the treatment of Cellulitis and Lymphangitis.

Hawthorn is one of the best tonics for the heart and circulation, balancing blood flow, pressure and heart rate. An important tonic for the performance horse with many added benefits, for a horse who is really brave and needs support or for the horse that needs extra "heart" after suffering a strain.

Rosehips is extremely beneficial for the circulation especially for the bridge between the arterial and venous circulation. A choice of circulatory herbs are always a valuable part of a mixture to treat disorders of the feet and legs.

JOINT ILL (SEPTIC ARTHRITIS)

Joint ill commonly occurs in foals but Septic Arthritis also occurs in adult horses usually as a result of a deep wound. Joints are swollen and painful, the horse or foal is severely lame and may also be depressed, off their feed and with a high temperature.

Herbs which have been seen to mitigate the effects of this blood condition include Guaiacum which is specific for the rheumatoid factor, reduces heat and friction in the joints and provides lubrication, Tansy also specific for the rheumatoid factor and Burdock which is a powerful blood cleanser, reducing heat, swelling and pain. Herbs for the treatment of osteo-arthritis will also be used as the bone is usually compromised as a result of the infection of the joint capsule.

Horse owners should seek professional advice in the treatment of most blood, circulation and lymphatic conditions as the selection of the correct herbs and dosage rates are quite critical in this area. Rosehips can however be used as a tonic herb routinely with complete safety. An excess of Nettles can cause "nettle rash", but just the right amount will bring out "dappling" on a horse's coat.

LYMPHANGITIS

Lymphangitis is usually a complication of a chronic infection and can be extremely serious if not properly resolved. It is an inflammation and infection of the lymphatic vessels in a limb. The lymphatic system is involved in removing excess fluid that has been created by infection and inflammation. Exercise stimulates the flow of lymph around the body so if there is pain and swelling in a leg, the horse does not want to put weight on it and the whole condition is aggravated. The combination of herbs I use to treat this condition includes herbs to stimulate the lymphatic system such as Fenugreek,

Clivers, Violet Leaves and Bladderwrack, the infection fighters Garlic and Echinacea, the anti-inflammatory and analgesic Devil's Claw and a choice of the circulatory herbs, Hawthorn, Rosehips, Nettles and Rue.

Selected natural feeds and supplements are vital to the healing of this condition as they are to long term general health.

If the lymphatic system of the horse is generally compromised, there will usually be a telltale swelling around the curved jaw line going upwards to the base of the ear. Cleansing and toning of the lymphatics can be achieved by using the herbs Fenugreek, Clivers or Violet Leaves for at least 12 weeks.

The lymphatic system is one of the body's defences against infection and keeping it in good condition is a sound preventive measure.

18 THE RESPIRATORY SYSTEM

"Researchers have found that the mechanics of the equine respiratory system impose a fundamental limit on how fast a galloping horse can breathe, which all the training in the world cannot alter." (2) The bio-mechanical linkage between stride and breathing means that the horse takes exactly one breath per stride in the gallop. "At high speeds the ratio of inhalation time to exhalation time in fact begins to drop. The horse simply does not have enough time to take in a full breath." (2)

This explains why "bleeding" is so common in racehorses, pacers and to a lesser extent in eventers and other competition horses.

"Bleeding" as it is known has other names - nosebleed, epistaxis, lung haemorrhage and exercise induced pulmonary haemorrhage. "The mechanical stress in the lungs which occurs with forceful breathing during exertion causes the delicate walls of the air cells to rupture, resulting in haemorrhage." (6)

A horse can quite easily have bled without there being blood coming out of the nostrils. Scoping provides the evidence. Bleeding severely impairs performance and even after long spelling, it may often return with the onset of fast work. Infection is a complication arising from the damaged tissue.

Herbal and Bach flower mixtures in association with adequate spelling have been seen to be very effective in repairing tissue damage and lifting infections out of the lungs. Treatment should commence as soon as there is any evidence of a bleed and should continue until well after the horse has resumed fast work. Rosehips, Elecampagne, Yarrow and Hawthorn are specific, while selected Bach flowers, nervine and demulcent herbs are just as important. Excessive use of chemical diuretics which is a fashionable remedy will more than likely cause further damage.

COUGHS AND COLDS

If a horse has a cough, it is important to ascertain the cause, so that appropriate treatment can be given. A cough is usually associated with a cold either of viral or bacterial origin or an allergy. It can also be associated with lungworm which horses pick up from donkeys. Sometimes horses can have an intermittent dry cough if the weather is very dry, which is usually not a cause for concern provided it resolves quickly. This can be assisted by adding 2-3 drops of Eucalyptus Oil to the water or molasses water used to dampen down the feed, but no more than that, or it may cause burning or irritation. Routine feeding of raw honey in the place of molasses is recommended for its anti-bacterial qualities.

The herb White Horehound is the one to use to alleviate symptoms of coughing and relieve irritation and inflammation. To break up phlegm Liquorice is specific. Demulcent herbs which are soothing to the throat and airways can also be used such as Marshmallow.

If the horse has a cold, cough or allergy affecting the respiratory system, Elecampagne is nearly always called for as it is antiseptic, soothing and will lift mucus and wastes out of the lungs so they can be coughed out.

The old faithful Garlic is always essential in the treatment of colds and for more serious conditions such as pneumonia for its antibiotic action, together with Echinacea to stimulate the immune system.

ALLERGIES

Horseradish is the herb to use for allergies affecting the upper respiratory tract like hay fever, also known as allergic rhinitis, together with Garlic and Chamomile. Euphorbia is a very useful herb in the treatment of all kinds of allergies including feed allergies, but dosage is critical so professional help is needed in its administration. For asthmatic types of allergies Elecampagne is again indicated and Grindelia which can relieve mechanical breathing difficulties.

LUNGS

If a horse is distressed to the extent that the normal breathing pattern has been interrupted, this may be serious and veterinary attention should be sought. See First Aid for how to check respiration rate. Many of the herbs already discussed are valuable in the treatment of lung problems, including pneumonia. Garlic is specific against Streptococcus which is often a cause of this serious condition.

INFECTIONS OF THE
UPPER RESPIRATORY TRACT

Abnormal discharge of pus and/or mucus from both nostrils is frequently associated with a cough. Herbal treatment to resolve the infection is led by Garlic and Rosehips, together with a selection from the herbs already discussed.

If there is a discharge of thick pus from only one nostril this is usually an indication of Sinusitis. This condition if it is not treated effectively and quickly can prove fatal. If it is chronic there will be a foul smell associated with the discharge which will probably be yellow. More than likely there will be lymphatic swelling around the jaw line, breathing may be difficult or noisy and there may also be facial swelling and pain. This condition may also be associated with a serious dental problem so it is important to have this checked as well.

Treatment includes the use of Garlic, Horseradish and Rosehips together with a selection from the herbs already mentioned in this chapter as well as treatment for the immune and lymphatic systems. Professional herbal help is essential.

The discharge is often so bad that the horse fouls its drinking water. The horse must be isolated and the water changed as often as necessary. The nostrils should be cleaned out with a mixture of lemon juice and water using clean cotton wool swabs each time. An inhalation using a tablespoon of Oil of Eucalyptus in a small bucket of hot water is also soothing and relieving.

A HANDY HOME REMEDY

This remedy can be used for horse and man for first aid as soon as symptoms of any respiratory infection, such as colds, appear. Ingredients - 6 whole lemons cut in quarters, 6 tablespoons of freshly chopped garlic, 1 knob of freshly grated ginger, a teaspoon of dried or fresh Thyme leaves, a pinch of Cayenne pepper. Method - Add whole lot to 3 litres (UK 5 ¼ pt; US 6 ½ pt) of water, bring to boil then simmer for 30 minutes. Dosage - For humans drink one small teacupful warm to hot, with a teaspoon of raw honey added, 6 times daily. For horses give two coffee mugs with each feed plus syringe 100ml of the cooled liquid directly into the mouth twice daily.

Management and nursing are of the utmost importance in the treatment of respiratory infections. Horses must be kept warm, comfortable, free of stress, out of the wind. Stables with good ventilation are essential.

THICK WINDEDNESS

Some horses are excellent in the wind, especially the "high blowers", but there are some horses which are a bit thick in the wind. Sometimes this can be due to lack of fitness if they are too fat on the inside, usually due to overfeeding. Pollard is the big culprit here. Post-viral syndrome can also affect the wind and herbal treatment for this is similar as for treatment of bleeders. Some horses do not breathe normally due to nervous tension - see The Nervous Horse. This also needs to be rectified with appropriate training.

"Roaring" is a condition caused by partial paralysis of the larynx (voice box) which affects a horse's ability to breathe normally. Veterinary diagnosis is made by scoping and surgery is usually successful. For horses which do not have to do fast work, it may not be necessary to operate. Some "roarers" do experience extreme nervous tension as a result of the condition, even if they are being used for lighter work and in these cases surgery may help relieve this complication.
A herbal treatment for the prevention and treatment of shock and stress due to surgery and to aid recovery would include Rosehips especially for its high Vitamin C content together with Rescue Remedy and any other herbs to suit the individual.

19 THE URINARY SYSTEM

The urinary system consists of the kidneys, bladder, ureters (tubes from kidney to bladder) and urethra (tube from the bladder to the exterior).

Keeping a check on your horse's waterworks should become part of good management. A reliable way of doing this is to teach them to urinate prior to work. I start by whistling the horse either in the stable or in some long grass after we have finished work. They are usually happy to comply at this time. After some consistent training they will urinate on the whistling cue prior to work at home or at a show. Apart from being able to keep a check on the quality of their urine, it makes the ride much more comfortable for the horse! This is also handy if you are worried a horse may be sick and you want to check this area. Being generally observant of their urinary habits is also a good plan which is made easier if the horses are stabled at night as they often urinate when they come in.

The colour of the urine should ideally be pale straw coloured, the same clarity and consistency as water. Abnormal colours - dark or bright yellow for example - may indicate insufficient water intake and/or high acidity. Milky or chalky urine is not such a problem as it is more likely to indicate alkalinity and horses on highly mineralised bore water may have normal urine this colour. Particularly offensive odours such as very strong ammonia may indicate insufficient water intake and/or high acidity. The same applies to urine which is thick and syrupy. However mares may produce this type of urine when they are in season. A foul smell from a sheath usually associated with an overproduction of smegma often indicates a urinary tract infection.

Difficulties in urinating such as straining or adopting the stance and then dribbling or not passing any urine, or too

many short urinations are usually signs of Cystitis (bladder inflammation and infection) or Urinary Calculi (stones).
A horse urinates on average from four to six times daily.

As the kidneys lie quite close to the top of the horse's back (the right just below the last 3 ribs and the left slightly further back), inflammation, tenderness and swelling may be detected in this area.

There are a number of antiseptic herbs which can be used to clear up urinary tract infections and Cystitis. Cornsilk is specific for mares while Clivers is specific for geldings or stallions. Uva Ursi is also useful for both sexes and all these herbs have soothing properties due to high mucilage. Couch Grass is also indicated especially if the flow is not strong and consistent. Parsley is a tonic herb for kidney function.

The herbs Celery and Juniper used together are excellent for removing acidity, providing a mild diuretic, encouraging horses to drink more and thus balancing hydration.
The common practice of using Epsom Salts routinely as a diuretic will damage the covering of the kidneys.

If kidney stones or gravel are suspected a diagnosis should be sought without delay from an expert equine veterinarian as giving diuretics may move small stones into a ureter and cause a blockage. This is extremely painful and can cause serious damage. There are herbs which can soften hard deposits such as gravel and small stones, so that they can be easily excreted. Apple cider vinegar in the diet is useful for prevention.

The urinary system maintains water and electrolyte balance in the body. The three main functions of water in the body are transport of nutrients and wastes, pH control and the dissipation of heat. The kidneys act as a filter excreting waste products of metabolism, particularly urea. They are a very resilient organ, being able to function even when considerably damaged. The opposite side of this fact is that optimising performance of the urinary system will have the same result in the horse.

Obviously then one of the most important ways to

maintain healthy kidney and bladder function is to ensure horses have ad lib access to generous amounts of clean, fresh water and then to be observant enough to be sure that they are drinking sufficient water. A horse needs to consume approximately 10% of its body weight daily in hot weather to maintain optimum water levels. For the average sized horse, 450kg (990lb), that is 45 litres (UK 100pt; US 124pt).

Water consumption is influenced by mineral content, contamination, automatic waterers and plastic containers. Horses may not consume enough water for balanced hydration if the water is not to their liking for whatever reason. Water quality is of prime consideration in keeping a high standard of health and to prevent urinary tract infections. See Water in The Magic Minerals and Vitamins.

DEHYDRATION

This is a common problem in performance horses. Even though horses are famous for their ability to sweat and therefore dump heat, there is a limit. "Getting rid of heat is not a limiting factor in most races, which last two minutes or less. But even moderately intense exercise that lasts much longer cannot be sustained without taxing a horse's thermoregulatory mechanisms to their very limit. The laws of physics that govern how quickly horses can get rid of the heat generated by their muscles impose an impenetrable ceiling on the upper limit of their performance in endurance races or other extended events. This is all the more so in hot and humid conditions, which undercut the effectiveness of the evaporative cooling mechanisms." (2)

Synthetic electrolytes are routinely given to performance horses and whilst electrolytes are obviously very necessary in many instances, excessive dosing when they are not called for can have a negative and overloading effect on the kidneys and the urinary system. Giving more and more electrolytes is not the answer to hydration balancing.

The important minerals in electrolyte balance - sodium, potassium, magnesium and calcium are easily provided as part of a natural feeding and supplements program. Sodium is provided by ad lib access to lumps of natural rock salt. Potassium is provided by apple cider vinegar, Calcium and Magnesium by high grade Dolomite. When it is necessary to get water and electrolytes into horses in a hurry, they can be offered tepid molasses water to drink. Molasses is high in Calcium and Magnesium as well as the B group vitamins. A tablespoon of Rock Salt can be dissolved in 10 litres (UK 17½pt; US 22pt) of molasses water. Apple Cider Vinegar can also be added at the rate of 40ml to the same volume molasses water for the provision of extra Potassium. Whilst most horses love to drink molasses water, some may not be so keen when the vinegar is added. A good general rate of dilution to offer molasses water is 1 tablespoon to 5 litres (UK 8¾pt; US 11pt) but this can be doubled to make it more palatable if really necessary.

Dandelion (Taraxacum Officinale) is high in Sodium, Potassium, Magnesium and Calcium and is a natural electrolyte. A good way to restore electrolyte balance quickly is to syringe Dandelion extract directly into the horse's mouth mixed with an equal amount of water. Dosage rate would vary from 2ml to 10ml depending upon the individual.

ANHYDROSIS OR "THE PUFFS"

This is a very serious condition where the horse is unable to sweat normally, which means it is unable to cool its body down and therefore cannot be worked. Characteristically anhydrotic horses will pant like a dog and become very distressed. The coat will stand on end.

The condition often occurs when horses are moved from

the more temperate southern climates to the hot and humid areas in the north, especially Queensland, the Northern Territory and the Asian countries. However horses which have been successfully moved north can develop the condition if they are over-stressed during hot conditions. In Queensland and the Territory, horses with anhydrosis can usually be worked in the winter months. Some horses eventually acclimatise in the summer while others do not and have to return south to cooler climates.

There are degrees of anhydrosis. There are plenty of horses in the more temperate climates who do not sweat freely and who also do not drink enough. These would be prime candidates for full blown puffs if they were to move into hotter and more humid climates.

I have been able to treat this condition successfully in some horses but only to a lesser degree in others. A combination of herbs to stimulate the sudoriferous (sweat) glands in the skin, gently stimulate the endocrine system as well as providing other herbs for the individual in question seems to be the answer. The Bach flower essences for prevention of stress and shock are also employed. This is a condition where professional help is essential. Careful attention to diet and training are also an important part of managing the problem.

NERVOUS URINATION

Some horses will urinate much more frequently than normal when they are feeling nervous and stressed. Routine feeding of Rosehips tea is ideal for these horses to prevent them from depleting their adrenal energy.

20 HORMONES, FERTILITY and GENETICS

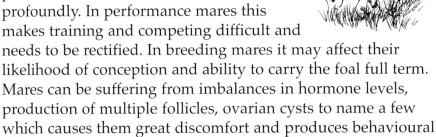

A lot of mares suffer from hormonal problems which affect their behaviour profoundly. In performance mares this makes training and competing difficult and needs to be rectified. In breeding mares it may affect their likelihood of conception and ability to carry the foal full term. Mares can be suffering from imbalances in hormone levels, production of multiple follicles, ovarian cysts to name a few which causes them great discomfort and produces behavioural difficulties.

Many mares, especially those who are in varying degrees of discomfort when they are in season, but who have regular cycles, may often be easily balanced using a short course of Chastetree Berry (Vitex Agnes Castus). This herb is used successfully for PMT in women and does not contain hormones.

Mares who have irregular cycles, who come into season at will or who are in season for long periods of time, need hormone balancing to normalise cycles.

Pokeroot (Phytolacca), an important general endocrine system herb and Sarsaparilla an endocrine system herb containing oestrogen, testosterone and progesterone are indicated for these conditions. Professional help should be sought in this area, as a short course is often effective.

For older breeding mares or mares who are difficult to get in foal or abort early without any apparent reason - a medium term treatment with Raspberry leaf several months before mating is likely to increase the likelihood of conception while strengthening the endometrium and uterus. Raspberry is the highest vegetable source of Folic Acid.

Mares with severe behavioural problems caused by

hormonal imbalances need to be diagnosed by a specialist equine veterinarian who will take blood tests to determine hormone levels and use an ultrasound to check the health of the ovaries and the reproductive organs. Professional herbal help can then be obtained to balance these mares with individually prescribed herbal and Bach flower mixtures.

The prevalent practice of putting a mare in foal to "sort her out" very seldom works. Double trouble can be the result. Even if the mental and physical problems disappear during pregnancy, they can very often reappear after the foal has been weaned.

Avoid feeding hay containing Red Clover to mares with suspected hormonal imbalances as it contains a high level of oestrogen. The herb Fenugreek should also be avoided for these mares for the same reason.

In fact pastures in which clovers predominate are contra-indicated for breeding stock. The hormonal imbalances which they can create may result in seriously impaired fertility.

PREGNANT MARES

There are a number of herbs which are contra-indicated for use during pregnancy as they have uterine stimulatory properties. They are Aloes, Devil's Claw, Parsley, Rosemary, Rue, Sage, Thyme and Wormwood. If you are feeding Garlic routinely to mares, delete it when they start to bag up as it may come through in the milk and upset the delicate digestive system of young foals. Reintroduce after the foal is about 4 weeks old.

FERTILITY FEEDS

Vitamin E and Zinc are important for fertility and nature has conveniently packaged them together in these feeds which are the highest sources - sunflower seeds, egg yolks, oats and wheat germ. Seaweed meal is also a source of Zinc.

If the nutrition of breeding animals is right in the first place, then problems will be minimised or avoided altogether. Unfortunately these days any country where modern chemical farming is practised suffers from induced mineral deficiencies in the soil, caused generally by the acidifying and/or inhibiting action of artificial manures and fertilisers. In Australia soil analyses from widely differing areas all show deficiencies in calcium and/or magnesium, sulphur and iodine to a greater or lesser extent. For these reasons much of the feed which we buy for our horses may be deficient in many of the necessary nutrients. Another effect of an imbalance in soil nutrients is that an excess of one will lock up others making them unavailable to the user. Therefore supplementation must be carried out. Fortunately nature does provide answers with substances such as high grade dolomite, seaweed, garlic, linseed, apple cider vinegar, natural rock salt and a great number of herbs which are nature's alchemists.

GENETICS

Unfortunately the practice of using mares "who are no good for anything else" to breed from is all too prevalent. Heritability of a whole range of problems is an accepted fact. Breeding for fads and fashions also has a severely negative effect on soundness.

Whilst some behavioural problems may not actually be genetically transmitted they are certainly passed through to progeny by example. Obviously a mare with a highly developed flight instinct is going to teach her foal to be the same. It is surprising how often one will hear of patterns occurring with various different traits.

Despite popular belief and practice, the mare is more important in the breeding equation than the stallion. There are

two reasons for this - the first, the maternal environmental influence, has been outlined above. The second is a scientific fact. "If there is any bias in the relative contribution of sire and dam in a given mating, it is in favour of the female.
The normal genes of the body are inherited equally from each parent. But the genes of one special part of the cell come solely from the mother. This is the organelle called the mitochondrion, a separate, self-contained part of the cell that is responsible for converting stored energy into work with the aid of oxygen." "Mitochondria are curious in another way, in that their DNA comes solely from the mother; there is no recombination of genes from both parents." (2)

There are a lot of famous horse breeders around the world who recognise the greater importance of the mare and use it to financial advantage.

The health of the mare at the time she is joined to the stallion is also of utmost concern to those breeders who want a healthy foal with the best start in life. Of course this is equally important in the case of the stallion.

The whole horse must be taken into account. The mare should be in excellent body condition, but not too fat, clear of infection of any kind however minor and in good spirits.
All the body systems, not just the reproductive system, and especially the immune system, should be in good health.
For instance, if the mare is a nervous wreck for whatever reason, she needs letting down so she can become relaxed before she is served.

Ideally the physical body and temperament should be balanced with herbal treatment over a full blood cycle (12 weeks) together with a natural feeding and supplements program to ensure the mare is as healthy and happy as possible prior to mating.

This will give her the best chance of delivering a healthy foal, with the best start in life. The principles outlined in the feeding chapters are all applicable to breeding stock.

THE ENDOCRINE SYSTEM

Hormones are the messengers of the glandular or endocrine system which is the control centre for all body activities. They are gland secretions carried in the bloodstream to the various organs.

Imbalances in any part of this complex system can therefore produce a wide range of symptoms. Blood tests are essential to pinpoint and diagnose actual disease such as tumours but may be inconclusive when it comes to minor imbalances.

There are many herbs beneficial to the endocrine system such as Pokeroot, but specialist prescribing is essential, in association with veterinary diagnosis.

An example of an imbalance of the endocrine system is hyper-thyroidism where the thyroid gland is over-active as opposed to under-active as in hypo-thyroidism. A goitre may be a symptom of both these conditions. It occurs underneath the base of the neck where it joins the jaws and is a movable, hard, round lump, not to be confused with lymphatic lumps or swellings which follow the base of the jaw where the neck joins and goes upwards to the base of the ear. An under-active thyroid gland is usually relatively easily treated with a good natural diet including seaweed. However horses with over-active thyroid glands will usually react badly to seaweed in the diet. They need to be balanced using prescribed herbal treatments. The herb Blue Flag is specific for thyroid balance.

A serious disease of the endocrine system is Cushing's Disease, which is a benign tumour of the pituitary gland, which controls all the other glands. Symptoms of this disease include a very long coat which does not fall out in spring or summer coupled with lethargy and weight loss despite increased appetite and water consumption. Veterinary diagnosis and treatment is essential and prescribed herbal treatments have been seen to be most beneficial and complimentary at any stage of this disease.

21 NATURAL
- NOT NECESSARILY GOOD

All the herbal remedies discussed in this book have been used successfully by me on my own horses and my clients' horses and are the result of my own training and experience. However, every horse is an individual and as such as they all react differently - so like everything in life there are no guarantees.

Just because a plant or substance is natural it doesn't necessarily mean it's good. Look at blue-green algae! There are many plants that are never toxic in nature at any stage - Dr Edward Bach called these "plants of a higher order". All his Bach flower essences are taken from such plants.

There are many plants that are toxic in nature - they do not have a place in legitimate herbal medicine. Some plants are only toxic if ingested in large amounts.

Some plants are toxic at a particular stage of their development and not at others, which is why it is not a good idea to go out wildcrafting unless you know what you are doing. A good example is the opium poppy. There is only a few days difference between the time the opium can be removed from the plant to the time the poppy seeds appear that we eat on our bread!

Some herbs are best used only externally for a variety of reasons. There are cautions and contra-indications in the use of many herbs. Dosage rates are critical with certain herbs and yet there are others where this is not the case. Do not fall into the trap of thinking "if a little is good, more must be better". The dosage rates that I use for horses are less than some herbalists use for people! Herbs are astonishingly effective in extract form at very low dosage rates - but only if the right prescription is worked out.

This book has been written to help horse owners use herbs, natural feeds and supplements as basic and preventive nutrition and for first aid, with the advice that they should consult me for medicinal treatments. It is not designed to take the place of expert equine veterinary attention, which is an essential part of responsible horse care.

DISCLAIMER

The information in this book is not to be used in place of veterinary care and expertise. No responsibility can be accepted by the writer or publisher for the application of any of the enclosed information in practice.

22 LIST OF USEFUL HERBS

ALOES - Aloe vera, A.. barbadensis, A.. socotrina, A.. capensis, etc

A succulent plant, member of the Lily family, but looks like a cactus. The medicinal part used is "the liquid exuded from the leaves of various species of Aloes, evaporated to dryness." (13) Very high in mucillage, hydrating for skin and bowels, muscle stimulant, anti-parasitic, demulcent, emollient, tonic and healing. Used for skin conditions, gut ulceration, worming, reversing dehydration and improving water intake. Must not be used internally on pregnant mares because of its muscle stimulating properties. Only use internally on professional advice or prescription. The species Aloe Vera is very easy to grow, recommended as part of your stable garden for external use. Scrape out the gel from the inside of the leaves and apply direct onto the skin of the horse to soothe and relieve bites, stings, blisters, welts and sunburn.

AGRIMONY - Agrimonia eupatorium

An alterative herb used for treatment of problems originating in the liver but also including kidney and spleen and the blood supply to these organs. It is particularly useful where the liver has been affected by poisons or other toxins including poisoning from feeds. Also as part of treatment for digestive problems, which result in scouring or other manure abnormalities. Use only on professional advice or prescription.

ARNICA - Arnica montana

The number one anti-bruising remedy, to be used externally in ointment form as quickly as possible after a blow to the body or legs where the skin is NOT broken, in conjunction with ice therapy. The herb is NOT used internally. For systemic treatment of bruising either alone or in conjunction with external treatment, homeopathic Arnica 6C can be administered internally without dilution. Bruising needs treatment just as much as open wounds - complete cleaning and repairing of the area prevents the possibility of weakness or worse still becoming a site for tumours or cysts many years later. A must for the First Aid Kit.

BLACK COHOSH - Cimicifuga racemosa

A powerful circulatory anti-spasmodic herb used for the internal treatment of recurring muscle spasm and to help with repair of muscle damage or injury. Use only on professional advice or prescription.

BUCHU - Barosma betulina

One of the many urinary system herbs, specially useful where cystitis or urethritis is recurring, Buchu is also good for shocked or damaged kidneys. It is quick acting and soothing also has specific endocrine system applications. A relative newcomer to western herbal medicine, it originated in Africa. Use only on professional advice or prescription.

BURDOCK - Arctium lappa

A powerful alterative and counter-irritant herb being very high in inulin. Extremely useful in the treatment of arthritis where the horse shows a rheumatism type of stiffness which is improved by exercise. Burdock is also diuretic and a blood purifier for skin problems like dry scurf, sores, boils and other breakouts. Can have a stirring effect on the bowels so it is wise to use internally only on professional advice or prescription.
A declared weed in Australia as the burr heads degrade the quality of sheep fleeces, it is eaten as a vegetable by the Japanese.

CALENDULA - Calendula officinalis

The common name is Marigold, but if you want to collect the petals and flower heads to make ointment, you need to make sure you have the right plant, the species Calendula officinalis and not the cultivars you see in the garden. Absolutely the number one antiseptic for treating cuts and wounds of all kinds. Use externally as a wash and in ointment form, it does not sting, is soothing and also has a restorative effect on tissues, removes inflammation, prevents scarring and restores nerve function. A must for the First Aid Kit in extract and ointment form. It should only be used internally on professional advice or prescription as dosage rates are critical.

COUCHGRASS - Agropyron repens

A urinary system herb with the specific use of toning sphincters or repairing bladders which are leaking for any reason. The rhizome is the medicinal part. Horses love to graze Couch Grass for its tonic properties. Very suitable for cutting as a fresh green feed for stabled horses.

CELERY - Apium graveolens

The seeds are the medicinal part of this herb which is well known as a salad ingredient. Invaluable as part of a mixture for the successful treatment of degenerative joint disease (osteo-arthritis) : as an alkaliser to help balance horses suffering from excess acidity in the tissues including tying-up: and to improve fluid circulation by encouraging the horse to drink more and sweat more freely. Nearly always used with its natural metabolic partner Juniper, together stimulating the Sodium / Potassium pump in the cells. Celery is high in Sodium as well as Chlorine and Silica while Juniper is high in Potassium. Celery is also a mild diuretic and urinary antiseptic with carminative (warming) effects, so is great for horses who have suffered a chill in the kidneys and often feel the cold.

Use Celery Seeds internally by making a tea from a good handful with 500 mls of water and use the whole lot to dampen down the feed to encourage drinking or to produce a warming effect.

CHAMOMILE - Matricaria chamomilla, Anthemis nobilis

An all time favourite and portmanteau herb, looking like a small daisy - the flowers are the part used. Chamomile is an important nervine, digestive, anti-arthritic, anti-allergy and anti-spasmodic herb.

Used for soothing, calming and relaxing nervous horses especially those prone to loose manure as a result, improves digestion, specific for scouring, treatment of osteo-arthritis, allergic conditions affecting the skin and respiratory system as well as for mild spasmodic colic. High in Magnesium Phosphate, Calcium Phosphate and Potassium Phosphates, Chamomile has a delightful aromatic odour.

Chamomile can be profitably used as a broad, general tonic herb for horses of all ages on a routine basis. Dosage - for preventive nutrition one handful dried flowers of Chamomile straight in the feed or made into a tea and the whole lot added, double the dose for arthritic and scouring horses. To soothe a horse with colic while you are waiting for the vet, syringe 100 mls of the strained, cooled tea with Rescue Remedy added every half hour.

External Use - As a wash to soothe irritated or itchy skin.

CHASTETREE BERRY - Vitex agnus-castus

This herb is used to treat PMT and menopausal problems in women. It is often the answer for mares who exhibit great discomfort and erratic, "bitchy" behaviour when they are in season, but who have a normal cycle pattern. It can also be used with other hormone balancers such as Poke Root or Sarsparilla, especially if the cycle is irregular or if the mare comes into season at will. This is a delicate area to balance and needs professional prescribing. Veterinary diagnosis utilising ultrasound and blood tests is also helpful. Usually treatment is only required for one cycle if Chastetree Berry is going to be effective on its own.

CLIVERS - Galium aparine

An antiseptic herb to resolve infection in the genito-urinary tract specifically for geldings and stallions, as well as providing soothing, anti-inflammatory and alkalising properties. Very high in Silica. Clivers is also a useful lymphatic system stimulant. Use internally on professional advice or prescription as there are many herbs used to treat the urinary system with many different specific applications.

COMFREY - Symphytum officinale

Comfrey is one of the most remarkable plants available for use in herbal remedies. One of its old fashioned names "Knitbone" explains its extraordinary ability to heal bone, but it has the same affect on cartilage, tendons, soft tissue, ulcers and wounds. This is partly due to is allantoin content which promotes replacement of the relevant cells at a much more rapid rate than in usual healing. This reduces the risk of scar tissue, proud flesh and arthritis.

The big caution with Comfrey is that it is not antiseptic. So in the early stages of wound treatment, especially very deep wounds and where there is infection present or suspected, antiseptic herbs, such as Calendula, must be used first, as well as raw honey. Comfrey is the highest plant source of Vitamin B12 and is very high in mucillage which makes it valuable to help heal gut problems such as ulcers. It is contra-indicated for use in young horses with osteo-chondrosis, even though it is very useful in the treatment of early arthritis patterns. Comfrey is still commonly used as a fodder plant for horses in Europe.

For details on how to poultice using fresh or dried Comfrey leaves see the chapter Understanding Herbs for Horses.

Comfrey leaves, either fresh or dried, can be fed to horses as an excellent adjunct to the external treatment. If fresh, only use the large, older leaves. One handful of dried or chopped, wilted leaves daily for an average sized horse (450 kgs). The use of Comfrey in the treatment of splints is outlined in the chapter on The Musculo-Skeletal System. How to make Comfrey oil from the milled root is outlined in the chapter on Understanding Herbs for Horses.

Bad press on Comfrey surfaces periodically and it is not allowed for internal use in humans in Australia. This is because of the presence of alkaloids which if ingested excessively over a long period of time are poisonous. These alkaloids are in higher concentrations in the root and young leaves. Comfrey's anti-tumour affects are due to its alkaloids. The noted British equine herbalist, Hilary Page Self, has this to say "My own feeling is that, like most things, if given in moderation as and when necessary, Comfrey presents no greater threat than any other herb and for external use there is nothing to touch it." Comfrey can be grown easily by striking small pieces of root taken from a live plant early in spring. It does not tolerate frost or too much hot sun and likes a lot of water. The old leaves are useful for activating compost because of the Vitamin B12.

CORNSILK - Zea mays

Another of the urinary antiseptics, Cornsilk, as the name

implies is made from the tassle of the corn, one of the few plants with medicinal uses that does not grow wild. It is specific for the treatment of cystitis, bladder irritation and irritable vagina in mares. Being very high in mucillage and with alkalising affects, it produces excellent symptomatic relief. The cause needs to be treated concurrently with other applicable herbs. Externally Cornsilk can be used as part of a douche mixture with Calendula, 10-15% diluted in water to relieve itching and burning.

DANDELION - Taraxacum Officinale

One of the portmanteau herbs, Dandelion is the great liver cleanser and tonic herb. The medicinal Dandelion (Taraxacum Officinale) must not be confused with the false Dandelion, also known commonly as Flatweed or Cat's Ear (Hypocheris radicans). The latter is associated with the onset of Stringhalt as is Capeweed. The medicinal Dandelion can be distinguished from the false Dandelion quite easily. Taraxacum Officinale has soft leaves (which are used for salad greens), and has flowers on a single stem. It grows only close to civilisation - in the garden, around stables and yards, in the lawn - it does not grow out in the paddocks. Cat's Ear has shiny, hairy and slightly succulent leaves which grow close to the round, has multiple flower heads with stems which divide and grows profusely out in the paddocks. Horses will only graze Cat's Ear for two reasons - either there is nothing else to eat OR they will deliberately seek it out even though they are on hard feed and grazing. The reason for this could be that they are trying to find minerals that are missing from their diet or they are trying to purge themselves. Horses should not be allowed to graze Cat's Ear and if they want to eat it, the reasons for this should be established and treated. I know of several cases of sick horses eating Cat's Ear. The medicinal Dandelion is NOT associated with Stringhalt. Dandelion is an alterative herb, liver tonic and cleanser, improves the metabolism, balances digestion and is also tonic for kidneys, spleen and bladder. It is high in Sodium,

Potassium, Magnesium and Calcium and is therefore useful as a natural electrolyte. It is also high in Choline, Iron, Silica, Sulphur, Vitamins A and D. Dandelion is used as a liver tonic, in the treatment and prevention of tying-up, detoxification, rehabilitation from illness and as part of a mixture to improve general health and wellbeing.

DEVIL'S CLAW - Harpagophytum procumbens

The major use of Devil's Claw is for its anti-inflammatory and analgesic properties especially in the musculo-skeletal system, so it also has applications in the treatment of arthritis and rheumatism. Regarded as the herbal alternative to 'bute', "tests carried out in Germany (one of the biggest users) have shown the painkilling and anti-inflammatory affects to be comparable with cortisone and phenylbutazone, without the attendant side-effects" (8) However in my experience there are times when the quick action of 'bute', for example in early stages of laminitis, is preferable, but only for short term use. For medium to long term use, for applicable conditions, Devil's Claw is the choice as it also stimulates healing. But as with any herb, it is not the whole answer on its own. Devil's Claw is not recommended for use in pregnant mares as it is a uterine muscle stimulant, or where gut ulceration is present or suspected.

ECHINACEA - Echinacea angustifolia, E. purpurea

Echinacea could be called the wonder herb of modern times, in great demand as a fighter of bacterial and viral infection, it is widely used as a disease preventative and immuno-stimulant. An alterative and antiseptic herb containing Copper, Cobalt and Iron as well as inulin and several fatty acids. Partnered with Garlic, this is a formidable front line against virtually all of today's antibiotic resistant infections as well as viral infections and also effective in the treatment of post-viral syndrome.

Echinacea angustifolia has recently been tested scientifically in relation to its efficacy in the treatment of horses by The Equine Research Centre in Canada. This confirmed that this species of Echinacea is an effective immune system stimulant in horses, significantly increasing the number of lymphocytes (white blood cells), whose job is to destroy invading pathogens. Interestingly these tests also showed an increase in the size and number of red blood cells and the level of haemoglobin in the blood from its use in horses.

ELECAMPAGNE - Inula

The number one antiseptic respiratory herb for horses, Elecampagne, is used in the treatment of all respiratory infections, coughing and allergies affecting the lungs. It is very helpful in healing weak and scarred lungs, to remove old infective material and mucus and as part of a mixture to treat bleeders. Soothing due to its high mucillage content, it is the highest plant source of Inulin and also contains Allantoin. This herb does not necessarily need specialist prescribing and can be profitably used together with Garlic, Echinacea and Rosehips.

EUPHORBIA - Euphorbia hirta

This herb must only be used on professional advice or prescription as dosage rates are critical. One of the best anti-allergy herbs it is useful to treat allergies affecting the upper-respiratory system such as hay fever and asthma, as well as allergic reactions on the skin such as acute itchiness, swelling and sensitivity from bites. Useful in treatment of acute or chronic conditions, results are generally rapid.

FENNEL - Foeniculum vulgare

A world wide weed which grows on waste ground, the seeds are the medicinal part. The root is a vegetable with an aromatic taste like aniseed. Specifically for the treatment of the pancreas, an organ vitally concerned with the metabolism, Fennel works wonders balancing horses with poor or voracious appetites and/or feed conversion difficulties and/or digestive problems. Needs specialist prescribing as it is usually given in association with a liver herb and often with lymphatic and digestive herbs to work properly. For obese horses the endocrine system also needs concurrent balancing. Fennel seeds can be employed as part of a herbal worming mixture.

FENUGREEK - Trigonella foenum-graecum

Better known as an ingredient in curry, where the powdered seeds are employed, Fenugreek is a legume which the Greek horseman used as a conditioning hay. It is an important lymphatic system cleanser and stimulant but is also tonic to liver, skin and digestive system. Fenugreek is almost identical in composition to Cod Liver Oil, being high in Vitamins A and D. It is highly nutritious containing lecithin compounds. Recommended as a feed herb to tempt picky eaters and improve general body condition, as part of a natural diet. The seeds are very hard so need to be soaked in hot water for few hours before feeding or fed as a powder. Start with a little and if the horse finds it acceptably gradually increase to 20 grams daily for an average sized horse (450 kgs) until the desired result is achieved. Fenugreek is high in oestrogen so do not feed it to mares who are in good to fat condition or who may have a hormonal imbalance, as it may produce flirtatious behaviour! Interestingly I did hear of one mare who had been given Cod Liver Oil whose behaviour changed in this way within 24 hours. Provided this caution is observed Fenugreek can be used as a general feed herb to keep the lymphatic system toned up. Fed in conjunction with Garlic, a very good two way bet to prevent infections.

GARLIC - Allium sativum

The most important of the portmanteau herbs, Garlic is a powerful alterative. It is a natural antibiotic with the huge advantage that it is selective and only kills pathogens. It is the greatest disease preventative and fighter being anti-bacterial, anti-fungal and anti-parasitic. " Garlic is effective against Staphylococcus, Streptococcus, Brucella, Salmonella and 9 other bacteria.... also roundworms, pinworms, tapeworms and hookworms .... and has proven anti-fungal properties including against ringworm." (4) Garlic is a storehouse of minerals the most notable being Sulphur, but also contains Zinc, Selenium, Iron, Copper, Chromium, Boron and Molybdenum. It's high Sulphur content cleanses the blood and deters internal and external parasites. Garlic is also a wonderful digestive herb maintaining balance of the gut flora. Garlic is fed worldwide to horses to prevent infections, especially respiratory infections. The only caution with Garlic is where a horse is scouring.

In severely chronic cases these horses may have a highly compromised liver function and or pancreas function, in which case Garlic should only be introduced later on in herbal treatment and not as part of the initial treatment. The taste test is valuable here - if the horse will accept Garlic offered by hand - it is safe to feed.

In human herbal medicine Garlic is a major cardio-vascular herb lowering blood pressure and cholesterol levels. Garlic either freshly crushed from the bulb or in dried granulated form should be fed to all horses on a daily basis. Two tablespoons daily for an average sized horse (450kg/990lb). Shelf life of the corms is extremely limited so it is better and easier to buy the dried granulated form which most horses find more palatable than the powder. Many feed stores now stock Garlic and it should only cost around Aus$7 per kg.

Garlic has been in use as a food and a medicine for 4000 years and is now in huge demand to fight anti-biotic resistant bacteria. In cases where a horse has an acute or chronic infection of any kind, please seek my help, as the extract form needs to be used in conjunction with other herbs, with special dosage rates, as quickly as possible.

GOLDEN SEAL - Hydrastis. External Use Only

The medicinal qualities of Golden Seal were discovered by the American Indians who used the root for bright yellow facial and body paint. From this cultural use they discovered that it cured their eye diseases. Golden Seal is most expensive as it has been overharvested and is becoming scarce in the wild. It's best use is in tiny quantities as part of an eye wash to soothe irritation from infection, dust or flies. See details in the chapter Understanding Herbs for Horses. As an ointment Golden Seal is antiseptic, soothing and drawing for skin pustules. The major caution is that it MUST NOT be used internally because of its extreme bitterness and powerful effects which will cause scouring.

GUAIACUM - Guaiacum officinale

Another of the wonderful alterative herbs Guaiacum is used

as a blood cleanser where the rheumatoid factor is present, such as in septic arthritis. Its other major use is to improve joint mobility as it lubricates, reduces heat and friction and has a beneficial affect on synovial fluid. It is therefore very useful in treating post-viral syndrome where the joints have been affected, including Ross River Fever. Must only be used on professional advice or prescription.

HAWTHORN - Crataegus

The berries and sometimes the leaves and flowers are used as a major heart and circulatory tonic. In human herbal medicine it is used to treat irregular heart beat, arteriosclerosis, heart shock and balance blood pressure. From the equine perspective it is valuable in the treatment of foot disorders such as navicular and laminitis. It is high in Rutin (Vitamin P) one of the bioflavonoid group with Vitamins K and C.

Their prime task in the body is to maintain the blood and adjust flow and constituents. Hawthorn therefore improves the circulation to the feet in particular, but it is also useful in the treatment of heart strain and bleeders. Needs specialist prescribing as other circulatory herbs such as Nettles, Rue, Rosehips may be preferable or combined.

HOPS - Humulus lupulus

One of the nervine herbs, Hops is one of the major ingredients in beer making and it is not coincindental that the old timers would often give their horses some beer as a gentle sedative or as a tonic. Already discussed in the chapter The Nervous Horse. Best given as a herbal extract rather than in beer form (because of all the chemical additives).

HOREHOUND - Marrubium vulgare

Excellent for the relief of coughing whether this is a dry cough or whether it is associated with a lower respiratory infection with irritation, inflammation and infection of the bronchial area. Best made into a tea, strained and used to dampen down the feed. As it is a very bitter herb, raw honey can be added which will also help if there is infection present.

HORSERADISH - Armoracia rusticana

Another herb which is a food and a medicine. Excellent for the treatment of hay fever in conjunction with Garlic. Add a dessertspoon of the powdered root to the feed in addition to your usual Garlic. Also add a handful of flowers of Chamomile. Maintain this treatment during the spring months. If not successful, seek my help for addition of other anti-allergy herbs. Horseradish is a valuable medicine in the treatment of sinusitis and inner ear infections but in these cases specialist prescribing is necessary because of dosage rates and herb combinations. Horseradish is also stimulating to the appetite and a pancreatic tonic.

HORSETAIL - Equisetum

A powerful alterative herb having the highest plant source of Silica. Also high in Magnesium, Phosphorous and Calcium. Invaluable in the healing of bone injury and in the treatment of degenerative joint disease. It strengthens bones and bone repair and is specific for structural faults and abnormalities such as spurs and chips. Must only be used on professional advice or prescription as dosage rates and specific applications are critical. Also used for abnormalities of the nervous system as opposed to nervousness. If your foals or horses are eating other horses' tails, they need Silica!!!

See the chapter The Magic Minerals and Vitamins.

JUNIPER - Juniperis communis

An important urinary system herb and diuretic, Juniper is usually used with its metabolic partner Celery to balance the Sodium/Potassium pump in the cells. Juniper is high in Potassium while Celery is high in Sodium. Together they balance fluid circulation and fluid waste removal through the kidneys. See Celery. Caution - Juniper should not be used if kidney gravel or stones are suspected - therefore specialist prescribing is necessary.

LINSEED (FLAX) - Linum usitatissimum

Linseed has valuable uses as an external raw oil and as a feed either boiled or fed as a cold pressed oil. Externally apply sparingly daily to retension contracted tissue especially tendons after trauma (or surgery).

See the chapter Are You Feeding Against Yourself?

LIQUORICE - Glycyrrhiza glabra

Liquorice has been used medicinally for over 3000 years and has been extensively researched in modern times.

It stimulates the production of cortisol in the body which makes it useful in the treatment of a wide range of skin conditions including itch. One of its main constituents glycrrhizin encourages healing of gut ulceration, but because Liquorice is also laxative and horses with this problem usually have very loose manure, there are other herbs which are more applicable. Liquorice is a great herb for coughs and colds as it loosens phlegm so it can be coughed out. Liquorice also has application in the treatment of adrenal exhaustion and in removing adhesions after foaling or surgery.

Caution - Liquorice should not be used in excessive doses or in the long term. Specialist prescribing is necessary. Holistic vets may use Liquorice in the treatment of impaction colic.

The Liquorice that is bought as a sweet these days is usually only flavoured with anise oil and not the real thing.

MARSHMALLOW - Althaea officinalis

From one old fashioned sweet to another! The medicinal uses of Marshmallow are in the treatment of digestive system disorders such as gut ulceration, inflammation, irritation, wind and bloat, where the high mucillage soothes the irritation thereby encouraging resolution and healing. "Powdered marshmallow root has been used as a preventative on horses prone to spasmodic colic." (8) A mixture of Marshmallow and Meadowsweet in the dried form can be added to the feed of horses who have any of the above difficulties as part of a natural diet. A good handful of each herb twice daily for an average sized horse (450kg/990lb).

Also see the chapter The Digestive System. However for chronic cases, I have found prescribed extract mixtures to provide a much quicker result.

MEADOWSWEET - Filipendula ulmaria

Another important herb in the treatment of digestive system imbalances, see the chapter Understanding Herbs for Horses under Synergy for a full description of this herb.
See Marshmallow above.

MUGWORT - Artemisia vulgaris

One of the important nervine herbs, Mugwort is used in the balancing of the nervous system as well as for the treatment of damage to the nervous system such as Stringhalt. See the chapter The Nervous Horse.

NETTLE - Urtica dioica, U. urens

The common old stinging nettle is a wonderful remedy for anaemia because it is very high in Iron as well as Vitamin C. Its actions are to raise the red cell count, improve oxygenation of the blood and to stimulate the arterial flow. In human herbal medicine they also raise the blood pressure, with obvious contra-indications, so are often partnered with Rue which balances the venous pressure with the arterial pressure. I therefore use these two herbs together with great care and in differing proportions to stimulate circulation in conditions such as laminitis, cellulitis and lymphangitis together with other herbs for detoxification. Specialist prescribing is therefore essential for these conditions. In the treatment of anemia the causes must be established and treated otherwise the symptoms will continue. Therefore while Nettle is usually indicated it needs to be prescribed with other herbs to treat the cause. Nettle can be used in dried form as a feed additive especially where green feed is needed (eg if a horse is intolerant of lucerne) as it is incredibly high in chlorophyll, or as a spring tonic to bring the new coat through more quickly and to encourage shine and dappling. Some horses may react with a nettle rash - if so, discontinue use. A handful of the dried herb once daily for an average sized horse (450 kgs) is adequate.

OATS - Avena sativa

In human herbal medicine Oats are used as a nervine and

heart tonic. And yes this is the same as the horse feed Oats, high in energy because of its starch and protein! The properties of Oats are to strengthen muscle after trauma and increase muscle bulk and strength. For this reason I often prescribe Oats in extract or tincture form for horses who have been injured or peformance horses who need to build muscle bulk and cannot tolerate Oats in the feed for whatever reason. See also Saw Palmetto.

PARSLEY - Petrolselinum crispum

A culinary herb, Parsley is useful in the treatment of anaemia as it also contains Copper in addition to the Iron and Vitamin C. It is essential in the rehabilitation of sick or injured horses together with a selection of other herbs which would probably include Sage and Yarrow. Parsley is supposed to have uterine stimulatory properties so do not feed to pregnant mares.

PASSION FLOWER - Passiflora

A nervine herb which is used in human herbal medicine to trigger the sleep centre in the brain. Has applications for horses and is discussed in the chapter The Nervous Horse.

PEPPERMINT - Mentha piperita

There are lots of different mints but they share the same constituents. A good feed herb which can be used to tempt picky eaters, to ease flatulence and to promote good digestion. A good handful of the dried herb daily added to the feed is sufficient for an average sized horse (450 kgs). Fresh mint of the culinary variety could also be offered.

POKE ROOT - Phytolacca

The number one glandular (endocrine) system herb, it should only be used on professional advice or prescription. It is a broad general tonic for imbalances in glandular function such as enlarged lymph glands and for regulation of hormone balance including reproductive functions.

RASPBERRY - Rubus idaeus

Raspberry leaves are traditionally used as a reproductive aid - to strengthen and tone the endometrium (lining of the uterus) and the uterine muscles and to increase the likelihood of conception.

This herb is the highest vegetable source of folic acid. For example Raspberry leaves can profitably be used for mares who habitually abort and bleed, for older mares who have had a lot of foals or for an older mare having her first foal. They should be given for at least one month prior to the mare being joined. A good handful of the dried herb can be added to the feed daily for an average sized horse (450 kgs).

RED CLOVER - Trifolium pratense

A powerful alterative, Red Clover is also a feed which can produce unruly results in some animals. Very high in Copper and Cobalt, it is affective against tumours and cysts and is also anti-fungal and anti-viral. It also has a strong ability to raise the red cell count in the blood. Used as part of a mixture to heal abscesses and prevent their return, to treat viral attack and post-viral syndrome and in stubborn cases of fungal attack such as greasy heel. Must only be used on professional advice or prescription. Red Clover as a feed or a herbal medicine may have oestrogenic effects on some mares, especially those with hormone imbalances, and also on some geldings or stallions.

ROSEHIPS - Rosa canina

One of the portmanteau herbs, Rosehips should be given as a feed herb as part of a natural diet. It is enormously high in Vitamin C as well as a vast array of other vitamins and a high mineral content including Copper and Cobalt. It is a broad general tonic, good for rehabilitation after any stress, illness or injury, an immune system booster, a circulatory herb especially beneficial to the bridge between the arterial and venous circulation which is one of the reasons it promotes strong, healthy hoof growth and is good for the health of the lungs. For high performance horses of average size (450kg/990lb) feed 2 tablespoons of Rosehips granules twice daily. To enhance the benefits, this can be made into a tea and the whole lot added to dampen down the feed. One tablespoon once daily is sufficient for pleasure horses and smaller horses or ponies. Rosehips in extract form is often part of mixtures to treat a wide range of conditions including bleeders, laminitis and infections.

SAGE - Salvia officinalis

A culinary herb, Sage has remarkable restorative powers. It is used as part of a mixture to rehabilitate very sick or injured horses, for nerve debility such as stringhalt and to improve concentration in nervous horses. Needs specialist prescribing. Do not give to pregnant mares.

SARSPARILLA - Smilax

An important alterative for the endocrine system especially in relation to sexual and reproductive areas. Very useful in balancing mares with disordered hormones including adrenal imbalances. Must only be used on professional advice or prescription as it has extremely specific applications.

SAW PALMETTO - Serenoa serrulata

This herb contains steroids and is therefore useful to strengthen and repair muscles after damage, weakness, wastage or paralysis, including hernias. However it is not recommended for use in mares as it may create erratic behaviour. See Oats as the alternative for mares. Saw Palmetto must not be used for prolonged periods of time. It can be used for under development of testes in colts and is also useful as part of a mixture just for a few weeks to lift a rundown horse.

SKULLCAP - Scutellaria lateriflora

An extremely useful nervine herb specifically for horses who adrenalise easily, characterised by nervous episodes where the heart rate rises and does not return to normal easily. See The Nervous Horse. Most definitely requires specialist prescribing as the dosage rate is extremely critical and too much may throw these horses into even more frenzied behaviour.

SLIPPERY ELM - Ulmus fulva, U. rubra

A must have for the First Aid Kit - both for internal and external use. Slippery Elm Bark powder is exceedingly high in mucillage and nutrients and is specifically indicated for scouring and the prevention and treatment of gut ulceration. It is soothing, mildly astringent and anti-inflammatory and given at the right dosage rates will not have the opposite effect. See Herbal and Practical First Aid. Externally it is good for poulticing as it is soft and sticky when water is added and can be used on its own or with other ingredients. Occasionally some horses will not readily eat the powder in their feed so they can be given the herb in extract form.

THUJA - Thuja occidentalis

For external use - essential for the First Aid Kit as an exceptionally effective anti-fungal ointment for treatment of greasy heel and for ringworms.
See the chapter Exterior Glow = Inner Health.

UVA URSI - Arctostaphylos uva-ursi

Commonly known as Bearberry, it is a urinary antiseptic to relieve inflammation and infection of the bladder and urinary tract. It is soothing due to its high mucillage as well as being astringent. Uva Ursi is also indicated if urinary calculi are suspected. It should not be used in the long term and if a horse has repeated urinary tract infections, seek professional help so that the causes are treated as well as the symptoms.

VALERIAN - Valeriana

An important nervine herb Valerian has been fully discussed in the chapters The Nervous Horse and The Holistic Horse.
Its anti-spasmodic qualities make it useful as part of a mixture for the treatment of tying-up and stringhalt. Because it is laxative it is contra-indicated for horses who have loose manure for any reason as it will make them worse.

VERVAIN - Verbena

A wonderful nervine herb with specific applications already discussed in the chapter The Nervous Horse. Vervain is an anti-spasmodic working on the surface circulation and in the peripheral nervous system. Also very useful as part of a mixture to treat bleeders.Thought to be a "cure-all" herb by the Greeks and the American Indians, it can be used as a feed herb for restorative effects after illness. A good handful of the dried herb once daily for an average sized horse (450kg/990lb).

VIOLET - Viola odorata

An infallibly useful herb for stimulating and cleansing the lymphatic system. Violet also has anti-cancerous properties and is used as a preventative and for treatment of melanoma in grey horses. Needs specialist prescribing.

WINTERGREEN - Gaultheria procumbens

For external use in oil form, only mixed with raw linseed oil and comfrey oil, Wintergreen is used for its penetrating and warming qualities. It has the extraordinary ability to penetrate up to 10 cms into tissue carrying with it the healing qualities of the other oils it is mixed with.
See the chapter Understanding Herbs for Horses.

WITCH HAZEL - Hammamelis virginiana

For external use only Witch Hazel is highly astringent and excellent for the treatment of bruising where the skin is broken. The commercial distilled product which you can buy in the supermarket is not nearly as effective as the extract which can be used straight, diluted as a rinse or as an ointment, depending upon the application.
See the chapter Practical and Herbal First Aid.

WORMWOOD - Artemisia cina

Wormwood is one of the most bitter herbs and is best used as part of a worming mixture. It must not be used on pregnant mares. "Artemisia cina, the Levant wormwood, is the real worm remedy, used not only against threadworms but also against roundworms." (4) See the chapter Herbal Worming.

YARROW - Achillea millefolium

The last of the portmanteau herbs, Yarrow is used internally and externally as the number one astringent.
It re-arranges fluid and blood loss internally and externally, is anti-shock and acts like a herbal suture on cuts and gaping wounds. It is protective, strengthening and supportive not only for physical wounds. Used as part of a mixture for very sick or injured and depressed horses, to strengthen the spine and in the treatment of many musculo-skeletal, hoof and foot problems. Yarrow has been used by soldiers since Roman times to staunch

wounds on the battle field. Easy to grow as part of your stable garden, the leaves and flowers can both be used. A good handful of the fresh or dried herb can be added to the feed daily for an average sized horse (450kg/990lb). A handful of the soft leaves can be used to hold on a wound with pressure to stop bleeding if you do not have extract on hand.

ST JOHN'S WORT - Hypericum perforatum

A nervine herb used to treat depression in humans, it is not recommended for internal use in horses because it causes de-pigmentation of the skin in cattle. Horses who suffer from photosensitivity would be at high risk. However it can be put to good use as an external oil to relieve itching on the skin from almost any cause.

See the chapter Understanding Herbs for Horses.

ST MARY'S THISTLE - Silybum marianum

A wonderful liver herb to be used when heavy detoxification work and liver cell regeneration is called for. For example when the liver is damaged from worm burdens, from long term drug use or from poisoning. Use on professional advice or prescription.

This list of useful herbs is by no means comprehensive. There are many other herbs that I also use - including Blue Flag, Capsicum, Elder Flowers, Gingko Biloba, Ginseng, Golden Rod, Grindelia, Hydrangea, Mistletoe, Pulsatilla, Rue and Tansy.

The most important thing to remember is that there is never just one herb that is going to be a quick fix for any horse. Deciding which herbs to use, for how long and in what proportions, is where the skill of the trained herbalist who has extensive experience of equines, is invaluable.

BIBLIOGRAPHY

(1) Healing Your Horse, Ihor John Basko DVM, Howell Book House, 1993

(2) The Nature of Horses, Stephen Budiansky, The Free Press, 1997

(3) The Complete Herbal Handbook for Farm and Stable, Juliette de Bairacli Levy, Faber and Faber, 1991

(4) Complementary and Alternative Veterinary Medicine - Edited by Allen M Schoen DVM and Susan G Wynn DVM, Mosby Inc., 1998

(5) Naturopathy for Horses, Gerd Emich, J.A. Allen, 1994

(6) Veterinary Notes for Horseowners, Capt. M Horace Hayes FRCVS, Stanley Paul, 1987

(7) Australian Horses as a Primary Industry - Bureau of Resource Sciences, Australian Government, Canberra

(8) A Modern Horse Herbal, Hilary Page Self, Kenilworth Press, 1997

(9) Dr Ian Bidstrup MVSc, Cert Vet Acu, Cert Vet Chir

(10) Sandy Parker, AFBA Accredited Farrier

(11) Andrew McLean, B.Sc., Dip.Ed., EFA/NCAS Level 2 Eventing Instructor

(12) Bach Flower Therapy, Mechthild Scheffer, Harper Collins, 1990

(13) A Modern Herbal, Mrs M Grieve, Penguin, 1980

General Bibliography

The Natural Health Book, Dorothy Hall, Penguin, 1976

Dorothy Hall's Herbal Medicine, Lothian, 1995

RECOMMENDED READING

- The Nature of Horses - Stephen Budiansky
- The Complete Herbal Handbook for Farm and Stable - Juliette de Bairacli Levy
- Veterinary Notes for Horseowners - Capt M Horace Hayes FRCVS
- A Modern Horse Herbal - Hilary Page Self
- A Modern Herbal - Mrs M Grieve
- Herbal Medicine for Horses Pages - Victoria Ferguson - Horse Deals Magazine published monthly
- Horses and Herbs Column - Victoria Ferguson - Hoofs and Horns published bi-monthly
- Horses for Courses Newsletter - Victoria Ferguson - published quarterly

USEFUL CONTACTS

AUSTRALIA

EQUINE HERBALIST

Victoria Ferguson
  Diploma Herbal Medicine
  Equestrian Federation of Australia Level 2
  Dressage Instructor
  Certificate of Horse Studies
  "Woodhurst", Largs, via Maitland NSW 2320
  Phone & Fax: (02) 49300128
  email: victoria.ferguson@herbalhorse.com
  Internet: www.herbalhorse.com
  Telephone Consultations - Australia and
  Overseas - Individually Prescribed Herbal
  and Bach Flower Mixtures, Natural
  Feeding and Supplements Programs,
  Herbal Oils/Ointments, First Aid Kits
  Feed herbs - Chamomile, Garlic,
  Rosehips, Natrakelp

Holistic Veterinary Association
  President - Dr Clare Middle BVSc, BVMS,
  Dip Acu, Dip Hom
  23 May St, East Fremantle WA 6158
  Phone: (08) 9339 7440; Fax: (08) 93398808

Royal Melbourne Institute of Technology
  Department of Chiropractic, Osteopathy
  and Complementary Medicine - For Vets
  and Chiropractors trained in Animal
  Chiropractic who treat horses contact Dr
  Fiona Kates, PO Box 71, Bundoora Vic 3083
  Phone: (03) 9925 7427

**Equus College of Learning and
Research/Equine Muscle Release Therapy**
  Equus College of Learning and
  Research/Equine Muscle Release
  Therapy™ (Bowen for Horses) - Director -
  Alison Goward, PO Box 151, Eumundi Qld
  4562. Phone & Fax: (07) 5442 8955
  email: emrt@ozemail.com.au
  Course Co-ordinator - Christine Pederson,
  PO Box 142, Stratford Vic 3862
  Phone: (03) 5145 6466 email:
  fullcircle@netspace.net.au

UK

The Dr Edward Bach Centre
  Mount Vernon
  Sotwell
  Wallingford
  Oxon OX10 OPX
  Tel : 01491 834678

**Equine Muscle Release Therapy -
Europe/United Kingdom**
  Sue Connolly
  Tel/Fax 01789 772413
  email - sueconnolly@lineone.net

HERB SUPPLIER

Larkhall Natural Health Inc
  Forest Road
  Charlbury
  Oxford OX7 3HH

USA and CANADA

**American Holistic Veterinary
Medical Association**
  2218 Old Emmorton Road
  Bel Air MD 21015
  Tel 410-569-0795
  Fax 410-569-2346
  email - 74253.2560@compuserve.com

HERB SUPPLIERS

Wide World of Herbs Ltd
  11 St Catherine St East
  Montreal
  Quebec H2X 1K3
  Canada

Indiana Botanic Gardens
  P O Box 5
  Hammond IN 46325
  USA

Nature's Herb Company
  281 Ellis St
  San Francisco CA 94102
  USA

Penn Herb Company
  602 North Second St
  Philadelphia PA 19123
  USA

INDEX

ALOE VERA

Chamomile

COMFREY

DANDELION

ECHINACEA

FENNEL

GARLIC

NETTLES

RED CLOVER

ROSEHIPS

E.GREEDY

WORMWOOD

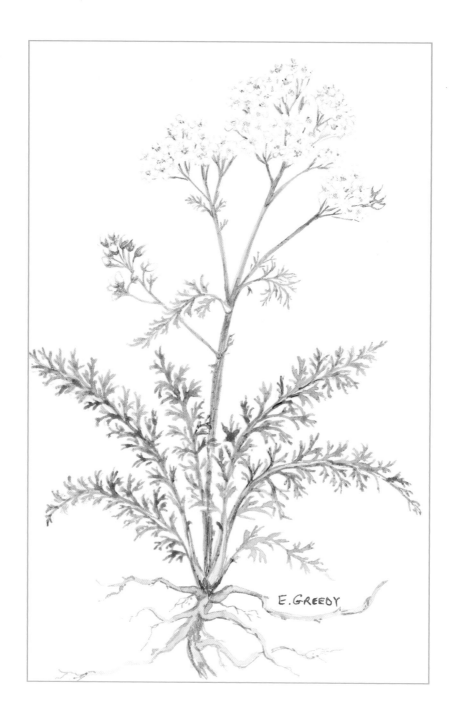

YARROW